SAVAGE REPRISALS

Bleak House

Madame Bovary

Buddenbrooks

Other books by Peter Gay

Schnitzler's Century (2001)
My German Question (1999)

The Bourgeois Experience: Victoria to Freud
Education of the Senses (1984)
The Tender Passion (1986)
The Cultivation of Hatred (1993)
The Naked Heart (1995)
Pleasure Wars (1998)

Reading Freud: Explorations and Entertainments (1990)
Freud: A Life for Our Time (1988)
A Godless Jew: Freud, Atheism, and the Making of Psychoanalysis (1987)
Freud for Historians (1985)
Freud, Jews and Other Germans: Masters and Victims in Modernist Culture (1978)
Art and Act: On Causes in History—Manet, Gropius, Mondrian (1976)
Style in History (1974)
Modern Europe (1973), with R. K. Webb
The Bridge of Criticism: Dialogues on the Enlightenment (1970)
*The Enlightenment: An Interpretation
Vol. II: The Science of Freedom* (1969)
Weimar Culture: The Outsider as Insider (1968)
A Loss of Mastery: Puritan Historians in Colonial America (1966)
*The Enlightenment: An Interpretation
Vol. I: The Rise of Modern Paganism* (1966)
The Party of Humanity: Essays in the French Enlightenment (1964)
Voltaire's Politics: The Poet as Realist (1959)
The Dilemma of Democratic Socialism: Eduard Bernstein's Challenge to Marx (1952)

SAVAGE REPRISALS

Bleak House

Madame Bovary

Buddenbrooks

PETER GAY

W. W. NORTON & COMPANY · NEW YORK · LONDON

For information about permission to reproduce selections from this book, write to
Permissions, W. W. Norton & Company, Inc., 500 Fifth Avenue, New York, NY 10110

The text of this book is composed in Fairfield
with the display set in Bauer Text Initials and Nuptial Script
Composition by Adrian Kitzinger
Manufacturing by The Courier Companies, Inc.
Book design by JAM Design
Production manager: Andrew Marasia

Library of Congress Cataloging-in-Publication Data

Gay, Peter, 1923–
Savage reprisals : Bleak house, Madame Bovary, Buddenbrooks / Peter Gay.
p. cm
Includes bibliographical references and index.
ISBN 0-393-05118-8
1. European fiction—19th century—History and criticism. 2. European fiction—20th
century—History and criticism. 3. Dickens, Charles, 1812–1870. Bleak House.
4. Flaubert, Gustave, 1821–1880. Madame Bovary. 5. Mann, Thomas, 1875–1955.
Buddenbrooks. I. Title.

PN3499 .G39 2002
809.3'0094—dc21   2002021874

W. W. Norton & Company, Inc., 500 Fifth Avenue, New York, N.Y. 10110
www.wwnorton.com

W. W. Norton & Company Ltd., Castle House, 75/76 Wells Street, London W1T 3QT

1 2 3 4 5 6 7 8 9 0

To Dorothy and Lewis Cullman,
who changed my life,
and to
Doron and Jo Ben-Atar
Jerry and Bella Berson
Henry and Jane Turner,
my New Haven crew

CONTENTS

List of Illustrations

frontispiece: *The Sword*, by Alfred Pierre Agache (1843–1915). Oil on canvas, Art Gallery of Toronto, Canada, 1896.

p. 34: "Charles Dickens at Desk with Characters." Original caption: "Author Charles Dickens surrounded by his characters." From a drawing by J.R. Brown. Undated illustration. Corbis.

p. 70: *Death Room of Madame Bovary*, by Albert August Fourie. Musée des Beaux-Arts, Rouen. Photo credit: Giraudon/ Art Resource NY.

p. 110: First edition of *Buddenbrooks* by Thomas Mann, 1901. Courtesy of S. Fischer Verlag.

The face of Dickens . . . is the face of a man who is always fighting against something, but who fights in the open and is not frightened, the face of a man who is *generously angry*, in other words, of a nineteenth-century liberal, a free intelligence, a type hated with equal hatred by all the smelly little orthodoxies which are now contending for our souls.

—*George Orwell on Charles Dickens (1939)*

For Flaubert, who all his life repeatedly declared that he wrote to *take his vengeance* on reality, it was above all negative experiences that inspired literary creation.

—*Mario Vargas Llosa on Gustave Flaubert (1975)*

But the only weapon available to the artist's sensitivity, to let him react with it to phenomena and experiences, to defend himself against them handsomely, is expression, is description. And this reaction by expression which (to speak with a certain psychological radicalism) is the artist's sublime *revenge* on his experience, will be all the more vehement the more refined his sensitivity.

—*Thomas Mann on Thomas Mann (1906)*

PROLOGUE

Beyond the Reality Principle

DURING THE SPECTACULAR CAREER OF LITERARY REALISM in the nineteenth century, the style was covered with accolades, none more heartfelt than Walt Whitman's: "For facts properly told, how mean appear all romances." Honoré de Balzac famously saw himself as "the amanuensis of history," a vaulting claim that the following pages will serve to examine and complicate, but which on their own convey a novelist's powerful sense of reality. And in February 1863, Ivan Turgenev brought word to fellow diners in Paris, all of them prominent literary figures—Flaubert was there, as were France's leading critic, Sainte-Beuve, and the Goncourt brothers, diarists and novelists—that Russian writers, too, a little belatedly, had joined the Realist party.

In fact, it is fair to say that well into the twentieth century, novelists across Europe and the United States were firmly committed to the Reality Principle. They made, as it were, a tacit compact with their reading public that obligated them to remain close to truths about individuals and their society, to invent only "real" people and situations, in short to be trustworthy in their fictions about ordinary life. Romantic sagas about gallant knights and improbable adventures, seductive ladies and doomed lovers, all bathed in extravagant luxury, were not for them. Rather, the Realists found their materials in circumstances essentially like their bourgeois readers' own styles of speech and ways of life. Even classic modernists like Marcel Proust or James Joyce created characters that, they insisted, obeyed the laws of human nature; in fact, *A la recherche du temps perdu* and *Ulysses* aimed at penetrating to the heart of internal life, the one with meticulous analyses and the other with linguistic experiments, more effectively than their more predictable fellow novelists could manage. Avant-garde or conventional, Realists made exceptional efforts to paint credible backgrounds and credible personages.

The three writers I am exploring in this book were all Realists, each in his own way. Their writings consistently paid homage to their commitment to the mundane. For all the eccentrics that populate Charles Dickens's novels, all his unsubtle division of characters into heroes and villains, he insisted in the strongest terms—in *Bleak House* perhaps most urgently—that he was in league with nature and science in imagining the scenes he spread out before his readers. Thomas Mann rifled his memories of Lübeck and canvassed his older brother Heinrich, other family members, and older acquaintances to provide his *Buddenbrooks* with the authority of living verisimilitude. Even Gustave Flaubert, who despised the newly fashionable genre called "Realism" for what he derided as its alleged vagueness and vulgarity, developed his own brand of Realism with fussy, downright obsessive care, making the characters in *Madame Bovary* as lifelike as possible. Whatever precise meaning authors, critics, and readers might assign to "Realism," they could agree that the serious novelist must strictly confine himself—and herself—to plausible characters living in plausible surroundings and participating in plausible (and one hoped, interesting) events.

But their increasingly prestigious vocation as novelists pushed leading Realists beyond the Reality Principle. They were makers of literature, not mere photographers or stenographers of commonplace life. Their prized imaginative powers liberated them in ways barred to scientists of society—sociologists, political scientists, anthropologists, historians—for whom facts and their rational interpretation remained paramount.* That is why nineteenth-century writers basked in the right to cherish their freedom from pedestrian constraints—of course always within reason. In the extraordinary letters that Flaubert wrote to his mistress Louise Colet at midcentury while he was at work on *Madame Bovary*, long bulletins from the front that amount to a treatise in aesthetics, he exclaimed over and over: "That is everything: the love of Art."

For his part Thomas Mann, astonished that *Buddenbrooks* should have caused "a sensation in Lübeck and bad blood," protested against this literal-minded reception of his first novel at home. "The reality that a writer subjects to his intentions," he wrote with some indignation of his own, "may be his daily world, may as a character be his closest and most beloved; he may show himself as subordinate as possible to details provided by reality, may use its deepest trait greedily and obediently for his text; and yet there will remain for him—and should for all the world!—an immeasurable difference between the reality and his handiwork: that is to say, the essential difference which forever separates the world of reality from that of art."

---

*In the pages that follow, I shall, for the sake of simplicity, use "historian" to stand for all these scientists of society.

This Realist manifesto is too eloquent to require much comment. There is no point in making excessive demands on the realism of Realism. Certainly, as Realist novelists and their readers knew perfectly well, Realism is not reality. At one point in *Buddenbrooks*, Mann propels the tale forward with the bridge passage, "Two and a half years later," a reminder that in fiction time makes acrobatic leaps. Again, late in *Education sentimentale,* Flaubert breaks into the continuity of his hero's life with a famous two-word paragraph, "He traveled," and then in a few terse words reports what happened to Frédéric Moreau between 1848 and 1867. The Realist novel cuts the world apart and puts it together again in distinctive ways. Its reality is stylized—pushed and twisted—to serve the requirements of an author's plots and character developments. Even when novelists deliberately resort to such easy, lazy tricks as the long arm of coincidence and the all-solving deus ex machina, they profess that the world they are constructing is authentic.

Realist fiction, then, to underscore the almost self-evident, is literature, not sociology or history. It permits, in fact invites, the pleasures of encountering Dickens's delightful or frightening misfits in *Bleak House;* observing Flaubert's dissection of a sadly overmatched provincial beauty in *Madame Bovary;* appreciating Mann's irony at play in *Buddenbrooks,* that most subversive of family chronicles. I have no quarrel with the literary critic who visualizes novelists, including those of the Realist persuasion, as alchemists who transmute the dross of the quotidian into the gold of art. Nothing I shall be saying in these pages should dissuade readers from taking novels as aesthetic productions with their own standards, their own gratifications, their own triumphs. After all, the novel is one of the signal achievements of modern civilization.

To be sure, there is more than one way of reading a novel: as a source of civilized pleasures, as a didactic instrument serving self-improvement, as a document opening doors to its culture. I have already singled out the first of these for praise; I leave the second, with its good intentions and its earnestness, to pedagogues and the salesmen of spirituality. In what follows, I shall investigate the third of these alternatives: this book is a study of novels as a possible (and possibly treacherous) treasure house of knowledge. That seems to me a necessary exercise, for it is by no means self-evident just how to extract truths from fictions.

LIKE OTHER READERS, MOST HISTORIANS HAVE IGNORED these difficulties, uncritically assigning or recommending novels as so many works of reference that supply dependable social and cultural information. True, no sensible scholar would turn to Franz Kafka's *Trial* for straightforward reporting on the Austro-Hungarian judicial system, or to his *Castle* for the duties of a land surveyor. But nineteenth-century novelists, particularly the Realist majority—like the Portuguese Eça de Queiroz, the French Goncourt brothers, or the American William Dean Howells—have seemed most promising as providers of serviceable particulars. Whether enshrined in laws or perpetuated by social habits like the authority of the father or the status of women in the family, the financial side of marriage arrangements, the average salary of a clerk, the correct mode of addressing a bishop, have been turned into bits of evidence that scholars have found attractive, almost irresistible.

Prospecting, say, for hard facts in Pérez Galdós's unforgettable novel, *Fortunata and Jacinta* (1886–87), which is set around 1870, a historian could come away with a mass of reliable information about bourgeois marriage in Madrid, intellectual fashions in university circles, prevalent business practices, and endemic political tensions. Again, the scholar interested in the history of the department store may do well to begin with Zola's *Au bonheur des dames* of 1883, after making allowances for some melodramatic overstatements and oversimplifications. Such examples illustrate why the novel seems such an unsurpassable guide. It stands at the strategic intersection between culture and the individual, the large and the small, rehearsing political, social, religious ideas and practices, portentous developments and epochal conflicts, in an intimate setting. Read aright, it promises to become a superbly instructive document.

The Realist novel is so rich in comprehensive implications precisely because it puts its characters through their paces across time and space as though they are real persons growing into a microcosm of their culture and its history. It treats them as individuals solidly anchored in their world, in *this* world. Justly so: by the age of five or six, a child is a miniature anthology of the ways of the society that envelops it. It has imbibed rules of conduct, canons of taste, religious beliefs from its educators formal and informal—parents, siblings, nannies and servants, teachers, priests, school friends. There is, after all, nothing astonishing about the fact that the child of Italians speaks Italian or the child of Episcopalians grows up to be an Episcopalian. By the time the youngster goes to school, then, after the first years of its domestic apprenticeship for life, it has learned, more or less effectively, how to deal with siblings, playmates, and authority figures, with competence and frustration, rewards and punishments, and the little hypocrisies necessary for survival. Realist novelists were bound to make their characters conform to such basic facts of life.

And early lessons persist, whether easily absorbed or obstinately resisted. This was no news to the Victorians; it had been no news to the ancient Greeks and to educators in the centuries from Plato to Pestalozzi. A hundred years before Freud made a theory of it, Wordsworth had famously proclaimed that the Child is father of the Man, and, in 1850, on his tour through the Near East, Flaubert mused in a letter to his mother: "First impressions are not effaced, you know that. We carry our past within ourselves; through our entire life, our wet nurse makes herself felt." A character first grown in the familial cocoon is unlikely to deviate from the course imposed on it in its earliest days.

Marxist literary critics have often complained that the "bourgeois" Realist novel fails to take sufficient account of the social location in which its personages must subsist and act. One of their leading theorists, G. V. Plekhanov, proposed that the critical reader of the bourgeois novel must translate the language of art into the language of sociology. But one need not be a disciple of dialectical materialism to recognize the incessant and intimate interaction of what I am calling the large and the small. Hawthorne wrote *The Scarlet Letter*, with its evocation of the unforgiving rigor of American Puritanism, without any ballast of literary theory. Dostoyevsky wrote *The Brothers Karamazov* without the benefit of Freud's account of the family triangle, the Oedipus complex.

As my exhibits will show, imagined characters pass (or fail) the tests the world imposes on them in their most private sphere, within the mind—responses to early mistreatment in *Bleak House*, marital disillusionment in *Madame Bovary*, fading fortunes in *Buddenbrooks*. All these personal reactions have their cultural dimensions. But the sole center of perceptions is always the individual, who tries to unriddle their meanings and to calculate their consequences. That is why it is possible, and can be highly productive, for students of society reading novels to oscillate between the large and the small, exploring each in the light of the other. The novel, in a word, is a mirror held up to its world.

BUT IT PROVIDES VERY IMPERFECT REFLECTIONS. Stendhal's famous definition of the novel as a mirror moving along a highway is arresting but incomplete: it is a distorting mirror. One of Dickens's mature works, *Hard Times*, published in 1854 right after *Bleak House*, may make this point for me. In the opening scene, he has a teacher, Thomas Gradgrind, address his pupils: "Now, what I want is Facts. Teach those boys and girls nothing but Facts. Facts alone are wanted in life. Plant nothing else, and root out everything else." With a sneer, Dickens calls Mr. Gradgrind, who injects his charges with this repellent doctrine, "A man of realities." As he pursues his argument, Dickens directs his most censorious and most bitter witticisms against what he considers the foundations of Gradgrind's pedagogy: the uncharitable, bloodless, almost literally inhuman philosophy of Jeremy Bentham and his followers, the Utilitarians; he apparently believed that this doctrine dominated and was ruining his England. "Coketown," Dickens's replica of an industrial city, is to his mind the perfect spawning ground for Utilitarians.

Acting as a prosecuting attorney, Dickens calls his witnesses to the stand, making them testify how horribly they have been disfigured by an education that trains the intellect and forgets the heart. Gradgrind's son, spoiled and irresponsible, takes his father's educational dogma far enough to end up a bank robber; Gradgrind's daughter, whose soul has never been permitted to blossom in her childhood and youth, defenseless and friendless, allows herself to be married to the well-named banker Mr. Bounderby, the richest man in Coketown, whom she does not love and cannot love.

This assault is not a serious critique of a philosophical school but a sheer lampoon. Whoever takes it to be a factual account would be misled almost as badly as are Mr. Gradgrind's charges by his Utilitarianism. Bentham's influence on English life in the decades of the 1830s and after was a complicated affair. An unsparing critic of the English law and encrusted English traditions, a radical committed to a psychology that put the calculus of pleasure and pain at its center, he had prominent disciples in Parliament and out who worked, at times successfully, to translate his ideas into legislation and administrative edicts. But Dickens was too emotional and too ignorant to appreciate the significance of Bentham's thought.*

For all these cautions, novels have much to say to historians. Even when they get things wrong, they may do so in instructive ways, throwing light on typical class attitudes or religious prejudices. Dickens, achieving unrivaled popularity with his often demagogic methods for attracting readers, seemed to speak to the longings for kindliness and justice among many of his contemporaries; Flaubert, maliciously misinterpreting the French bourgeoisie, gave voice to the anxieties of a literary and artistic

---

*In his fine study, *The Dickens World* (1941; 2nd ed. 1942), Humphry House writes: "Many people still read Dickens for his records and criticism of social abuses, as if he were a great historian or a great reformer" (p. 9). Of course, he was neither. As for his critique of Utilitarianism: "It is impossible to say that he disliked Bentham's theories, because there is no evidence that he knew what they were" (p. 38).

avant-garde appalled by middle-class tastes; Mann, half lamenting and half caressing the decay of the German patriciate, offered
perceptive insights into the ravages of drastic social upheavals. Yet
whoever enlists fiction to assist in the hunt for knowledge must
always be alert to authorial partisanship, limiting cultural per-
spectives, fragmentary details offered as authoritative, to say nothing of neurotic obsessions. That is why the reader who treats a
novel as rich in clues to social, political, and psychological insights
must always consult second opinions.

THERE IS ONE TYPE OF REALIST FICTION THAT MAKES
particularly stringent demands on its author and its readers alike:
the historical novel, notably the kind that includes historic players in its cast of characters. Hadrian, Robespierre, Napoleon, van
Gogh, Bismarck, both Roosevelts, Stalin, even Elvis Presley—the
list is endless—have found their way into novels, often as protagonists. When writers enlist these outsized personalities as instru-
ments of their political enthusiasms or aversions, as they have
often done, their novels yield little if any new historical wisdom.
They only dramatize what readers have already learned elsewhere
or lay bare their inventor's take on politics.* The authors of historical novels must struggle between fidelity to undisputed biographical facts and the flights of their literary imagination. Certainly

---

*See Gore Vidal's *The Golden Age* (2000), which makes the long discredited view
that President Roosevelt provoked the Japanese attack on Pearl Harbor a cen-
terpiece. In this instance, the novel becomes a political diatribe rather than "reliable" historical fiction.

readers must grant novelists some leeway as they make up their protagonist's conversations and thoughts, but the boundaries that hem them in as they imagine words and ideas for which they have at best limited warrant must remain narrow. If they violate them, they make a Bismarck or a van Gogh into a tool of ideology or of fancy, into a largely fictional figure that happens to bear the name of, and somewhat looks like, a real person.

Inventing reality is a demanding business. It is like filling in a mosaic from which some of the pieces are missing and others are illegible. There can be no general rule just how much fictional passages are legitimate reconstructions, and how much sheer fancy. Certainly the leeway for imagining the conduct of real persons inhabiting a novel must vary with the writer's skill and information. To the gifted and well informed, much is permitted. In an author's note to her massive and persuasive novel on the French Revolution, *A Place of Greater Safety* (1992), Hilary Mantel candidly points out: "The events of the book are complicated, so the need to dramatize and to explain must be set against each other."* This is the conflict the historical novelist must resolve. Mantel does her best—which is very good—to stay close to the dates, places, and import of historic events and to derive her principal portraits—of Robespierre, Danton, Desmoulins, Marat—from what she could discover about them. But, following her major characters into their youth and their intimate relationships, she had to go beyond what she could actually verify. And it is in these imaginary intervals (which she took care not to make too imagi-

---

*"The reader may ask how to tell fact from fiction," she adds. "A rough guide: anything that seems particularly unlikely is probably true." This is amusing and, considering the excited times her novel deals with, not wholly implausible. But it cannot be taken as a general rule (p. x).

native) that she had to take her audience with her. The test that *A Place of Greater Safety* passes, not as a novel but as a piece of imagined history, is that a historian specializing in the French Revolution can read it without cringing.

Readers want to trust writers of fiction quite as much as they think they want to trust historians. At a price higher than usually imagined: the infamous hunchback of Richard III, which everyone takes to have been the ultimate cause of his viciousness, should stand as a warning against credulity. It was fabricated by a talented Tudor propagandist named William Shakespeare, quite incidentally showing how clever concoctions have a way of smuggling themselves into our sense of the past, how fiction becomes "fact." But, just as readers like to trust writers, for their part too makers of fiction want to be, or at least seem to be, worth trusting. The burden on the Realist historical novelist to earn that trust is particularly onerous.

A LOOK AT *WAR AND PEACE* MAY SERVE TO ILLUSTRATE the genre and its problems. Even as a young rake, Tolstoy was an avid and largely self-started reader, and when in 1865 he launched *1805*, which was to grow into *War and Peace,* he prepared himself diligently. He studied memoirs, letters, autobiographies, and histories, and consulted knowledgeable archivists. His principal sources were bulky histories then fashionable, like Adolphe Thiers's vastly detailed, and vastly popular, *Histoire du consulat et de l'empire* (1845–62), a liberal interpretation of the recent French past that supported the French Revolution until its time of Terror, and Napoleon before he became a bloated world conqueror. Its twenty volumes were a treasure trove for Tolstoy, and he pillaged them freely.

In short, he had an enormous amount of historical material at his disposal, much of it quite authoritative; in consequence, many of his crowded pages withstand skeptical scrutiny. Tolstoy actually insisted that he could document each of the events he chronicled down to the slightest detail, a dubious claim at best. More, he was obsessed by a radical theory of history: Great men are playthings of forces they do not recognize and could not overcome if they did. Truth lies not in the pompous pronouncements of celebrities but in the sayings of humble peasants or the sage conduct of blunt, honest soldiers who let the spirit of their country speak through them. Hence, to Tolstoy, Napoleon, the very embodiment of vanity who believed that his actions changed things, was a most pathetic puppet in the hands of history. Hence, too, Tolstoy remodeled Prince Kutuzov, the Russian commander in chief during the French invasion of Russia in 1812, from a courtier into a wholly admirable spokesman for Russia's soul.* Tolstoy's philosophy of history, as he called it, is an interesting perspective, but what matters here is that Tolstoy allowed it to override some of the information at his command. If facts contradicted his thesis,

---

*Tolstoy had "an undisputed right," writes Isaiah Berlin, in *The Hedgehog and the Fox* (1933), "to endow [his heroes], Pierre Bezukhov or Karataev [the wise peasant] with all the attributes he admired—humility, freedom from bureaucratic or scientific or other rationalistic kinds of blindness. But Kutuzov was a real person, and it is all the more instructive to observe the steps by which he transforms him from the sly, elderly, feeble voluptuary, the corrupt and somewhat sycophantic courtier of the early drafts of *War and Peace* which were based on authentic sources, into the unforgettable symbol of the Russian people in all its simplicity and intuitive wisdom." Once this transformation is complete, "we have left the facts behind us, and are in an imaginary realm, a historical and emotional atmosphere for which the evidence is flimsy, but which is artistically indispensable to Tolstoy's design. The final apotheosis of Kutuzov is totally unhistorical for all Tolstoy's repeated professions of his undeviating devotion to the sacred cause of the truth" (p. 28).

Tolstoy would sacrifice the facts. Acceptable as much of the novel is as dramatized history, it is just as well that people read *War and Peace* as literature.

IT FOLLOWS FROM ALL THIS THAT ANYONE EVALUATING the evidence a novel might provide must get to know intimately not just the fiction in question, but its maker and his society. To borrow from Kipling: What do they know of novels who only novels know? To understand what fiction has to offer the researcher, he must learn what made it happen. That is why the essays that follow will embed fictions in the literature and politics of their time, and in the author who gave them their being.

There are (to put it schematically) three principal sources of motivation—society, craft, and individual psychology. These are not watertight compartments but flow into one another, making the act of literary creation an intricate process. It is only together, in unique, not wholly predictable proportions, that they produce a portrait, a statue, a tragedy—a novel. Only a third- or fourth-rate work can be largely explained by a single cause: a hack writer spurred on by the profitable demand for his stories; a lifeless epic by the superior models its author has shamelessly appropriated; an amateurish first novel by its author's compulsion to regurgitate early memories. To make literature of any distinction, the sublimation of intimate motives calls for more mental exercise than this. It must command the often conflict-ridden cooperation of the causes I have listed: the novelist's society, the novelist's craft, the novelist's mind.

In this trio, the last, the psychological springs of action that include unconscious wishes and anxieties, do double duty. For what must ultimately have the greatest impact on the novelist is not simply what really happens in his (or her) culture but what he makes of it, not simply what his profession really demands of him but how he receives or reshapes its canonical procedures. This may sound like an attempt on my part to impose a psychoanalytic reading on a writer's work. But while I am sympathetic to, indeed engaged in, this line of interpretation, I fully recognize that it is not without its hazards. Whether it fosters or obstructs literary understanding depends on the claims made for it. It is one thing to characterize George Eliot's *Silas Marner* as a wishful attempt to master the traumas of her life—which, in part, it seems to have been—quite another to parade this partial analysis of the novel as a sufficient interpretation, precluding the need for more investigation. All simple, one-dimensional readings, the Freudian among them, are susceptible to the crippling and uninteresting formulations we disdainfully call "reductionism."

IT WAS PRECISELY THE CHARGE OF REDUCTIONISM THAT modernist writers began to level against the Realist novel after the end of the nineteenth century. Searching for techniques that would capture the complexities of human nature at work more satisfactorily than Emile Zola or Theodor Fontane to their mind ever had, masters like James Joyce in *Ulysses*, Marcel Proust in *A la recherche du temps perdu*, Virginia Woolf in *Mrs. Dalloway,* and lesser authors in their camp experimented with syntax, points of view, internal monologues, and bold offenses against the King's English and other didactic norms.

These innovators, of course, were also Realists in their own way; the Realist novel has never disappeared. But they expanded the range of what they thought belonged to the realities open to the makers of fiction. The Old Realists, too, had claimed to understand the motives of their protagonists, but their exposition was largely indirect, allowing readers to deduce minds through actions. In contrast, the New Realists dug beneath the surfaces of behavior. Just as the novelist's mind is an indispensable element in any exploration of his work, so the minds of imagined characters require careful scrutiny. Hence the second opinions to which their audience could appeal were far less from history than from psychology. The Old and the New Realists belong to the same literary universe, but what divides them is equally important.

No novelist has confronted this gulf more lucidly than did Virginia Woolf. In a famous paper, "Mr. Bennett and Mrs. Brown," that she delivered before friends in 1924, she pleads for the kind of Realism that does not remain content with the social surfaces of fictional characters. Everyone knows that essay, or at least quotes her observation that "on or about December 1910, human character changed." She mentions changes in "religion, conduct, politics, and literature," but it is the last of these, literature, that really concerns her. The leading Realists of her day gave her no satisfaction. She quotes Arnold Bennett, her principal target: "'The foundation of good fiction is character-creating and nothing else,'" and wholly agrees with him. "I believe that all novels . . . deal with character, and that it is to express character—not to preach doctrines, sing songs, or celebrate the glories of the British

Empire, that the form of the novel, so clumsy, verbose, and undramatic, so rich, plastic, and alive has been evolved."

But Bennett's way of creating character, she objects, fails to carry out the contract he has, as it were, made with his readers. She chooses at random one of his novels, *Hilda Lessways,* and documents her contention: the eponymous heroine's creator speaks extensively about the town she sees from her window, goes into detail about the house in which she lives and the rent her mother pays. That, she insists, is the wrong way, an impoverished, stunted Realism. This is not to say that she views nineteenth-century novels as invariable failures. There have been great writers like Tolstoy from whose *War and Peace,* it seemed to her, "there is hardly any subject of human experience that is left out." She is not arguing that a novelist must be a modernist to meet her stringent demands for a Realism that is as deep as it is wide.

For the student of Realism in Dickens, Flaubert, and Thomas Mann, this reasonable agenda comes as a relief: we may wonder if Dickens, one of the greatest of caricaturists in any literature, is as penetrating with human reality as he believed himself to be. As we shall see, this is a difficult issue, for there are ways to truth through exaggeration. But, as the pages that follow will demonstrate, with the authors of *Madame Bovary* (which Virginia Woolf includes in a short list of great novels) and of *Buddenbrooks,* there can be no doubt. They, and Dickens, give the historian much work to do, especially the historian not afraid of Freud.

ONE

THE ANGRY ANARCHIST

CHARLES DICKENS IN

Bleak House

IF THERE WAS ONE CRITICAL MOMENT IN HIS NOVELS that was Charles Dickens's specialty, and that unfailingly appealed to the Victorians' ready tear ducts, it was the emotional death scene. And in *Bleak House*, he disposed of several characters in particularly satisfying ways. There is likable and obstinate young Richard Carstairs, who dies of a broken heart as his fantasies of quick riches evaporate. There is Lady Dedlock, the heroine's mother, who is found dead near her lover's grave. There is Jo, the ragged, illiterate crossing sweep, whose demise gives Dickens a golden opportunity to denounce his heartless fellow citizens. But none of these can rival the sudden exit of Krook, the coarse, mean-spirited owner of a wretched junkshop, who shuffles off his mortal coil by collapsing into dust. This particular death did not play on the reading public's love of a good cry but on its credulousness. Krook's end, Dickens expected his vast readership to believe, was a case of spontaneous combustion.

He did not take all his public with him, and some skeptics among them went into print with their objections. G. H. Lewes, a prominent editor and literary critic, and, as the companion of

George Eliot, an intimate of genius, declared that "spontaneous Combustion is an impossibility." Instead of letting the matter drop, or conceding that disposing of a fictional character in this fanciful fashion was just an amusing literary conceit, Dickens energetically defended himself. In his preface to *Bleak House*, he marshaled eighteenth-century experts to show that about thirty cases of authenticated spontaneous combustion were on record. "I have no need to observe," he assured his admiring audience, "that I do not willfully or negligently mislead my readers, and that before I wrote that description I took pains to investigate the subject." That his authorities were anything but authoritative seems not to have occurred to him. When one thinks of Realists in nineteenth-century fiction, one does not think of Dickens first, but he wanted it known that he had reality firmly in his grasp.

He took the same strong line justifying his portrayal of Nancy, the prostitute, in *Oliver Twist*. When Thackeray accused Dickens of knowing full well that "his Miss Nancy is the most unreal fantastical personage possible," and that he "dare not tell the truth concerning such young ladies," Dickens countered testily in a preface to the novel, "It is useless to discuss whether the conduct and character of the girl seem natural or unnatural, probable or improbable, right or wrong. IT IS TRUE." He apparently assumed that writing in capitals, as it were shouting in print, could substitute for reasoned debate. There was something at stake in this squabble: in depicting a whore with a heart of gold, Dickens's fiction was in danger of being lumped with the popular lowbrow English genre called the Newgate novel, which idealized criminals and turned them into heroic outlaws. But even if this contempt by association had not hung over Dickens, he would have sturdily stood for the verisimilitude of his characters and their fates. THEY ARE TRUE.

In a curious way, one personage in *Bleak House*, Harold Skimpole, supports Dickens's assertion that his fictions were drawn from facts. Though not a central character—a few reviewers thought him gratuitously dragged in—Skimpole, like everyone in the novel, is a pawn necessary to the plot. He is a master sponger forever pronouncing himself to be a child who lives for poetry and music alone and to whom money means nothing. He lives off other people who are so charmed by his sprightly conversation that they are willing to overlook his unscrupulous exploitation of his friends and his family.

Some readers singled out Skimpole as one of Dickens's most "delicious" characters, but those in his circle readily recognized the portrait as a brutal caricature of Leigh Hunt. An agreeable poet, liberal essayist, and prolific playwright, Hunt's main contribution to nineteenth-century English letters was his work as an editor. He knew everybody in the literary world and launched many a reputation in his periodicals, including that of Keats. He was perpetually short of money, what with a large family, an alcoholic wife, and the meager income his magazines provided. The vicious narcissist Dickens invented for *Bleak House*, though, was the very opposite of Hunt in almost every respect except his impecuniousness. As a minor concession, he instructed the illustrator of *Bleak House*, Hablot K. Browne ("Phiz"), to draw Skimpole as short and stout: "singularly unlike the great original," since Hunt was tall and slender. But this disguise was too perfunctory to hoodwink anyone in Dickens and Hunt's crowd.

Certainly, Dickens was sure that he had got Hunt absolutely right. In a confidential letter of September 1853 to a friend, Mrs. Richard Watson, he boasted about his portrayal of Skimpole: "I suppose he is the most exact portrait that ever was painted in

words! I have very seldom, if ever, done such a thing. But the like-
ness is astonishing. I don't think he could possibly be more like
himself." He announced that he would not do such portraits again,
but in Skimpole "there is not an atom of exaggeration or suppression. It is an absolute reproduction of a real man. Of course I have
been careful to keep the outward figure away from the fact; but
in all else it is the Life itself." About six weeks later, he reaffirmed
his borrowing from life in a letter to an aggrieved Hunt: "everyone
in writing must speak from points of his experience, and so I of
mine with you."

Whatever the cause of Dickens's resentment may have been,
his conscience smote him. Writing to Hunt in early November
1854, he explicitly denied what he had explicitly affirmed before.
"The character is not you, for there are traits in it common to fifty
thousand people besides, and I did not fancy you would ever recognize it." In a word, feeling guilty about his savage treatment of
his old friend, he could think of nothing better than to lie to him.
On this occasion at least, his claim to be a truthful Realist had
even more substance than he was willing to admit.

2

BUT FOR DICKENS, REALISM WAS NOT SYNONYMOUS WITH
literalism. Starting with the opening scene of *Bleak House,* with
its famous evocation of the London fog, he enlisted a notorious
fact of metropolitan life as a metaphor to make a political point.
"London. Michaelmas Term lately over,"—this is the first sentence
of the novel—"and the Lord Chancellor sitting in Lincoln's Inn
Hall. . . ." Then, in an apparent leap: "Fog everywhere. Fog up the

river . . . fog down the river, where it rolls defiled among the tiers of shipping, and the waterside pollutions of a great (and dirty) city." These two realities are not distinct: they describe a single phenomenon. If any doubt should remain, Dickens resolves it promptly: "at the very heart of the fog, sits the Lord High Chancellor in his High Court of Chancery."

Serious readers of *Bleak House* have long recognized that Dickens gave the fog connotations far wider than its usual meaning. It was a savage comment on the irrational rigidity, the willful obscurantism, that the Court of Chancery embodied for him and that he saw spreading across London like a blight. And, though this is less evident than will appear in the course of the novel, the Court itself is a stand-in for one of Dickens's favorite villains, the Law. "The law," says Mr. Bumble in *Oliver Twist,* "is a ass—a idiot." The Dickens of *Bleak House* intensified this negative appraisal: the law was worse than stupid; it was vicious.

Dickens was never subtle about his symbolism. What with London's chimneys belching out deadly particles from coal-burning stoves and fireplaces, the fog was real enough. But its impenetrable gloom, its lethal emanations, its intermittent omnipresence ideally served a writer intent on pointing the finger at larger evils— evils that Dickens, the intuitive and impetuous reformer, was determined to expose, even, in his most ambitious moments, to eradicate. The fog, in fact, had served him before. In November 1850, he had written an article in *Household Words,* the periodical he had launched earlier that year, in which he openly employed it as a commanding metaphor. "Mrs. Bull and her rising family were seated round the fire, one November evening at dusk, when all was mud, mist, and darkness, out of doors, and a good deal of fog had even got into the family parlour." Unfortunately, that parlor was not fog-proof, though the Bulls did have an excellent ventilator over the fire-place. Its name: "Common Sense." Nothing could be more obvious.

THERE IS MORE THAN ONE WAY TO START A NOVEL. Its author may plunge into the action by introducing the protago-nist. "Call me Ishmael," we recall from *Moby-Dick*. "For a long time I used to go to bed early," is Proust's way of launching his ser-pentine river of a novel. Dickens, too, at times adopted this tech-nique. "Whether I shall turn out to be the hero of my own life, or whether that station will be held by anybody else, these pages must show," is how he introduces *David Copperfield* and David Copperfield, both the novel and its protagonist. But not in *Bleak House*. He begins not with individuals—we cannot count the Lord Chancellor as a person; he is a figurehead draped in the habili-ments of authority—but with the public stages on which Dickens will unfold his drama: the Court of Chancery and its own larger backdrop, the city it disgraces. He pushes without delay into the heart of the matter for his characters, which he sees also as a great matter for his country: the abuse of authority, the law's delay. Hanging over all the personages in the novel is an appalling, seem-ingly immortal legal tangle, "JARNDYCE AND JARNDYCE."

In short, the reader is made to feel in painful detail the pres-sure that social forces exert on individuals. Dickens deploys the small and the large, the interplay of personal destinies and social issues, with impatient rapidity. The novel, as crowded as a nine-teenth-century grand opera with its stars and teeming with spear carriers, is (whatever its detractors have said) beautifully con-trolled. Each character, major and minor—even, as I have said, Mr. Skimpole—contributes to the tale. And Dickens's fog dramatizes the pervasive presence of society, which profoundly affects, often permanently enslaves, its victims.

Mr. Jarndyce, of the unfortunate family enmeshed in the suit that bears its name, can partially rise above the case. As a philanthropic gentleman who spends his days assisting those less fortunate, he has been made to suffer less than the impecunious casualties of the interminable affair. The young wards in Chancery, the beautiful Ada and her beloved Richard, both of whom Jarndyce virtually adopts, do not fare so well. The two fall in love and secretly marry, but Richard, in company with so many others in the Court's grip, grows addicted to his suit. Defying all evidence, he refuses to see it as a beckoning, mendacious mirage, and constructs a fantasy kingdom in which his case will be settled promptly, greatly to his financial advantage. Ada's affectionate and increasingly desperate entreaties fail to shake him loose from his delusion, and he dies almost literally of *Jarndyce and Jarndyce*.

Others ensnared in the Court's web also suffer recurrent bouts of irrational buoyancy. Krook, he of the spontaneous combustion, seems remote from the Jarndyce imbroglio, but has papers that he thinks might be profitable to him in the case. Among the more marginal characters, perhaps the saddest is a genteel and pathetic elderly madwoman, Miss Flite, who faithfully attends every session of the Court, predicting to all who will listen a favorable outcome of her suit any day now. There are others broken by the Law, destroyed by hopes they would have had—under normal circumstances—every right to cherish. But, Dickens insists, the Court of Chancery is wholly incompatible with normal circumstances.

To be sure, like all of these cases, *Jarndyce and Jarndyce* does benefit some participants in this cruel play: the lawyers. They batten on their hapless clients by arousing expectations they know

full well the Court will never gratify—the attorneys and barristers
are among the most chilling presences in *Bleak House*. At long
last, after years and even decades, once a case is finally settled, it
often happens that there is nothing left for the heirs; the whole
estate will have been absorbed by costs—that is, absorbed by the
lawyers' fees. Others in the novel, like Mr. Snagsby, the nervous,
timid, softhearted stationer who supplies all the paraphernalia necessary to a lawyer's practice, profit in a far more modest way. Yet
Snagsby, too, will be drawn into the crowded panorama that daz-
zled Dickens's readers in 1852 and 1853, installment after monthly
installment. Snagsby employs men with a legible hand to do copy-
ing for his clients, and one of these is a destitute, silent, enigmatic
law writer who soon dies and seems to disappear from the narrative. Yet it will emerge that he had the closest connection to
another domain of English society so distant from Mr. Jarndyce's
circle as to seem beyond reach, let alone intimacy.

For *Bleak House* moves in two worlds, and Dickens does not
linger in introducing his readers to the second of them. The chapter "In Fashion" follows directly upon the first, "In Chancery." It
features Sir Leicester Dedlock, Baronet, in his late sixties, very
class-conscious, intellectually limited, rather pompous, anxious to
see the Old England he loves being subverted by so-called reformers. He is, though, sincerely attached to his wife, Lady Dedlock,
at least twenty years younger than her husband, still beautiful,
unfailingly elegant, remote, self-contained, and ostentatiously
bored. The couple move restlessly from their country estate to their
town house and back, or flee to Paris in search of entertainment,
accompanied by relatives and hangers-on, all of them, whether
rich or much reduced in income, fearfully fashionable.

It is self-evident that Dickens would not have placed his novel in two widely separated social spheres if he had not planned to join them somehow. And, far more than the obscure law writer of whom readers get just a glimpse, it is the protagonist, Esther Summerson, who unites the two worlds. Significantly, Dickens introduces her as the narrator of the novel's third chapter, closing the circle. She too, like Ada and Richard, is an orphan whom the munificent Mr. Jarndyce invites to make her home with him. Eventually, she will be revealed to be Lady Dedlock's illegitimate daughter, and the law writer her father. As the narrator of thirty-three of the novel's sixty-seven chapters, she is privileged to meet, and closely observe, almost everyone in *Bleak House,* and participates in the progress of its convoluted narrative. Unlike heroines in several other Dickens novels, she is active; even, with all due modesty, opinionated. She survives maltreatments, disappointments, and diseases, and will end up marrying Allan Woodcourt, an idealistic young doctor who worries more about his patients than he does about himself. It is the interaction of the two spheres, and Esther Summerson's growth into deserved marital felicity, with *Jarndyce and Jarndyce* long a looming presence, that are at the core of *Bleak House.*

MANY READERS HAVE FOUND ESTHER SUMMERSON a stumbling block to a full enjoyment of the novel. She is simply inhumanly perfect. She is devout, discreet, modest, loving, hard-working, pretty, preternaturally perceptive. "I had always rather a noticing way," she confesses as she introduces herself. She harbors no wicked thoughts even for those who have mistreated her. She quickly charms everyone she meets: rough working-class men, their oppressed wives, gentryfolk, the sick, the eccentric, the mad, and, of course, children. She is, though inexperienced and untrained, an imaginative, reliable housekeeper for Mr. Jarndyce, importantly clanking her bunch of keys, superintending supplies, regulating expenditures. Perhaps not surprisingly, her elderly guardian falls in love with her and proposes marriage, an invitation to a dull domestic quietness untroubled by sexual excitement that she gratefully accepts even though she loves someone else. Unable to appreciate her many virtues to their full extent, she has to be pushed to claim her true preference after Mr. Jarndyce comes to his senses and hands her over to Woodcourt. " 'Allan,' said my guardian, 'take from me, a willing gift, the best wife that ever a man had.' " All he wants from the couple-to-be is an occasional invitation to the house he also bestows on them. "Let me share its felicity sometimes, and what do I sacrifice? Nothing, nothing." This is the sort of passage that makes even a loyal Dickensian cringe.

That is simply too much virtue to pile on a single mortal; such pure creatures exist only in the fantasies of men who have never got over their boyish vision of their mother as a Madonna, and who have carried this idealization into adult life. To be sure, some contemporary reviewers delighted in Esther's sweetness. John Forster, as Dickens's closest friend scarcely an unbiased witness, particularly admired the early portions of her narrative, "as charming as anything Mr. Dickens has ever written—indeed some of the best things in the book." Other Victorians, more tough-minded, did not care for her—there *were* far more tough-minded men and women among the Victorians than they have been credited with. G. H. Lewes listed Esther Summerson among Dickens's "monstrous failures." An anonymous reviewer in the *Spectator,* out of patience with the parade of her admirable qualities, also demurred: "Such a girl would not write her own memoirs, and certainly would not bore one with her goodness till a wicked wish arises that she would either do something very 'spicy'; or confine herself to superintending the jam pots at Bleak House." Another, in *Bentley's Miscellany*, found her, like Mr. Jarndyce, quite unreal, and objected sensibly enough to the way that her guardian surrenders her to Woodcourt: "We do not know whether most to marvel at him who transfers or her who is transferred from one to another like a bale of goods."

Recent critics, too, have declared her "mock modesty" to be quite "tiresome." And it is true that Dickens's most impassioned admirers have felt compelled to acknowledge that his pathos— implausible unselfish actions, prolonged and heart-rending death scenes, the cozy munificence of philanthropists—too often lapsed into bathos. Yet, even though some mid-Victorians anticipated twentieth-century reserve toward Esther Summerson, there was a shift of emotional responses from their day to ours. What has struck recent readers as involuntarily funny in Dickens, many among his contemporaries thought immensely moving. Reading about Jo's last minutes on earth, they, like Oliver Twist, asked for more. Oscar Wilde's famous quip that one must have a heart of stone to read about the death of Little Nell in *The Old Curiosity Shop* without laughing was more than a typical perverse witticism: it signalized the emergence of a new, a more cynical post-Victorian sensibility. Characters in *Buddenbrooks* are strangers to such sentimentality, and the one character in *Madame Bovary* who exhibits all its symptoms pays for it.

READING ABOUT ESTHER SUMMERSON, THAT MODEL OF flawlessness, one must remember that she was not an isolated or uncharacteristic leading character in Dickens's oeuvre. She had a sister in Agnes Wickfield, the heroine of *David Copperfield,* the novel that directly preceded *Bleak House.* The character of Agnes says much about Esther Summerson, especially since many of Dickens's readers—certainly this reader—regard *Copperfield* as his finest novel, a judgment that Dickens shared: he called it his "favourite child." It is an English *Bildungsroman* which, particularly in its first half, strikingly resembles the author's own youth. It chronicles a thriving writer's life from his birth to his thirties, happily married and a happy father—a denouement Dickens liked to provide for his heroes and heroines even though (or, rather, because) his own marriage was quite unhappy. Agnes is Copperfield's second wife, after a brief marriage to Dora, an appealing, girlish young woman who providentially dies to give way to her successor, who has been his affectionate "sister" since childhood and who is his destined mate. David Copperfield needs to mature, to educate his heart, before he can truly value the treasure he has in Agnes.

From the first, Agnes's angelic traits irritated some of Dickens's vast audience. Reviewers accused him of producing a mere cipher, a Victorian doll lacking all individuality. Some called Agnes "detestable." Even the almost invariably supportive John Forster admitted in his biography of Dickens that he preferred Dora, Copperfield's "loving, little child wife," to Agnes, with her "too unfailing wisdom and self-sacrificing good." And in the twentieth century, George Orwell, in an appreciative essay on Dickens, said almost the last word on that model of womanhood. Agnes, he wrote, was "the most disagreeable of his heroines, the real legless angel of Victorian romance." After so devastating, so confident a verdict, what hope for an appeal?

Part of this indictment has merit. It is true that the personage who persists in calling Agnes an angel is David Copperfield, a fictional character. But there is every sign that Dickens subscribed to the adoring words he invented for his protagonist. We have seen it over and over: the subtly nuanced character was not his strong suit; he discovered the urge to oversimplify, to exaggerate, to caricature, too enticing. His villains are so very villainous, not just in their actions but in their appearance, that the reader almost expects to find drops of blood on the page. When he came to human types he detested—sectarian preachers, orotund hypocrites, sadistic authority figures—he could satirize them so broadly as to descend to sheer lampoons. No wonder that Henry James, that subtlest of writers, had strong reservations about Dickens, to his mind "the greatest of superficial novelists." Sir Leicester Dedlock, in *Bleak House,* is a rare and gratifying exception: after his wife flees as her murky past is about to be exposed, this stuffy, reactionary, empty-headed aristocrat shows himself to be a man of authentic decency. He refuses to think ill of the woman who has left him, and keeps hoping—we know that it is in vain—that she will return to him. But for the most part, there are angels in Dickens's novels and devils, or, to put it less dramatically, wholly benevolent and wholly malevolent characters.

Yet for all of Dickens's melodramatic streak, I want to offer two pleas on Agnes Wickfield's behalf, the one psychological, the other cultural. Agnes's mother had died in giving birth to her, and her father, a charming, weak-willed lawyer given to drowning his sorrows in drink, perpetually revisits this calamity, this fatal fact of his, and his daughter's, life. One can safely predict the effects of such tactless reminders. Agnes lives with her father's accusation every day, even if it does not sound reproachful, only mournful. And children are bound to take any family discord upon themselves. They will feel responsible, even guilty, when parents quarrel and, worse, when a mother dies in childbirth, especially when one has been the agent of her demise. To put it bluntly: Agnes Wickfield stands convicted of murdering her mother.

Hence, when her father proposes to take his clerk, the power-hungry, fawning, and repulsive Uriah Heep, into partnership because he has fallen under his baneful influence, Agnes confides to her "brother" David that, facing down her anxious qualms, she has advised him to carry out his plan. The reason? A wan hope that this gesture will give her "increased opportunities" of being her father's "companion." She begins to weep—it is the first time he has seen her lose control: "I almost feel as if I had been papa's enemy, instead of his loving child. For I know how he has altered, in his devotion to me. I know how he has narrowed the circle of his sympathies and duties, in the concentration of his whole mind upon me. I know what a multitude of things he shut out for my sake, and how anxious thoughts of me have shadowed his life, and weakened his strength and energy, by turning them always upon one idea. If I could set this right! If I could ever work out his restoration, as I have so innocently been the cause of his decline!" It is a poignant, accurately observed speech. Her father, self-pitying and, in the guise of concentrating his attention on his only child, totally self-absorbed, has convinced Agnes that he has made all his sacrifices for her sake alone. By telling her, however delicately, that she has been "the cause of his decline," he insinuates that it is her task to set things right—a labor of Sisyphus. Being utterly neglected would have been less damaging to Agnes than this pointed solicitude. She was so ineffably good, in a word, because she feared that she was unspeakably bad.

My plea for Agnes also has a cultural dimension, for it is essential to remember that Dickens did not reveal, or intend to reveal, the attitudes that respectable Victorian women had toward erotic experience. They were far from the sexless creatures they have traditionally been accused of being. To be sure, there was widespread prudery, much embarrassed evasiveness about the pleasures and risks of Eros among Victorian bourgeois. But there were also middle-class young women who went into marriage passionate creatures, or those who soon learned to match their husbands in enjoying the marital intercourse of which they had had only most indistinct impressions—often quite wrong ones—during their virginal years. The endlessly repeated jokes about the frustrated nineteenth-century husband and his frigid wife have some evidence on their side. But they do not document a bourgeois culture in a perpetual state of sexual malaise. Given all the hush about sexual life in Dickens's novels, the reader might be forgiven to assume that his married couples produced children by means of parthenogenesis or osmosis. But such humor is at once cheap and deceptive; it equates public silence with anxiety and with feelings of guilt. The Victorians drove the middle-class obsession with privacy to its extremes, and believed that the bedroom, in which its deeply personal secrets were enacted, must remain off limits to prying eyes. But it is a serious misreading of whatever evidence has survived to believe that bourgeois Victorian couples did not freely practice, or did not greatly enjoy, what they did not talk about.

THESE CONSIDERATIONS FULLY APPLY TO ESTHER Summerson. I have called her and Agnes Wickfield sisters; they might have been twins. Like Agnes, Esther had suffered a guilt-inducing childhood. The caretaker she called "godmother" who raises her and who, it will emerge, is her mother's sister, is utterly devout—she goes to church three times on Sundays and to morning prayers two days a week—and utterly gloomy. "She was a good, good woman!" Esther recalls. "She was handsome; and if she had ever smiled, would have been (I used to think) like an angel—but she never smiled. She was always grave, and strict. She was so very good herself, I thought, that the badness of other people made her frown all her life."

Unfortunately, the "other people" whose badness this "good, good woman" thought worth frowning over prominently included her ward. On one of Esther's birthdays, the pious godmother exclaims: " 'It would have been far better, little Esther, that you had had no birthday; that you had never been born!' " Upon hearing this declaration, Esther breaks down in tears and begs her godmother on her knees to tell her something about her mother. " 'What,' " she asks, giving voice to her childish conviction that somehow everything is her fault, " 'what did I do to her?' " Grimly, her godmother relents after a while. " 'Your mother, Esther, is your disgrace, and you were hers.' " And she advises the " 'unfortunate girl' " before her, " 'orphaned and degraded from the first of these evil anniversaries,' " to forget her mother. Then, as if this were not enough, she adds, " 'Submission, self-denial, diligent work, are the preparations for a life begun with such a shadow on it. You are different from other children, Esther, because you were not born, like them, in common sinfulness and wrath. You are set apart.' " Hardly a welcome birthday greeting.

Esther, weeping, retreats to her room and reports to her doll, from which she has no secrets, what has happened. And she resolves "that I would try, as hard as ever I could, to repair the fault

I had been born with (of which I confessedly felt guilty and yet innocent) and would strive as I grew up to be industrious, contented and kind-hearted, and to do some good to some one, and win some love to myself if I could." Precisely like Agnes, she was intent on mending her flaws, even if, whatever she thought them, they were not hers. I should add that at the end of the novel, Esther enjoys a kind of gentle revenge against her darling Ada, though she could not have been aware of it. For Ada, still her closest friend, has remained a widow, while she, Esther, has been blissfully married for seven years. She has two little daughters, while Ada has a son, named Richard after his father, but no husband.

It is by no means certain that Dickens was aware of his psychological penetration. If not, his insight into Esther's (and Agnes's) deeper motives is uncanny. Esther, the young criminal, grows up ridden with daunting feelings of shame and remorse, astonished that anyone should like, let alone love her, disposed to belittle her looks, and inhibited far beyond the measure of shyness that middle-class morality considered normal for young women of her class. Largely internalizing the world's view of her— and for years her "godmother" is her world—she refuses to rage against it even though it had dealt her such a bad hand.

That is why, a little queasily, she agrees to marry John Jarndyce even though, as we know, she yearns silently for someone else, and her prospective husband is about three times her age. The tribute that her early years exacted from Esther Summerson was steep. On this point, she is once again much like Agnes. For Agnes too, even more persistently than Esther, had kept locked in her breast her dearest wish: to become David Copperfield's wife. It is only after he proposes to her that she tells him that she has loved him all her life. All this, to say nothing of the thousands who clam-

ored for the monthly installments of Dickens's novels, helps to
account for the unspotted virtuousness that so many of Dickens's
more sophisticated readers have found disagreeable, improbable,
downright alien to human nature. They strongly preferred
Thackeray's scheming Becky Sharp to the paragon Esther
Summerson. True, even Dickens, that writer most committed to
respectability, could at times break out of the common pattern:
Victorian social habits virtually prescribed that the man take the
initiative in asking for a woman's hand. Yet he has Florence
Dombey, in *Dombey and Son,* ask Walter Gay to marry her. It is a
rare moment in Dickens, not a move that Esther, or Agnes, would
have found thinkable.

DICKENS ALSO HAD PRESSING PRIVATE REASONS FOR
idealizing his heroines. There are some interesting clues that point
to his problematic relationships with women, starting with his
mother. Problematic relations with women have of course been a
common experience among men since Adam was seduced into sin
by Eve. But Dickens's conflicted, never resolved feelings on this
fraught subject deserve special attention, for they emerge, trans-
figured, in his angelic females.

All of Dickens's biographers, whether eager or hesitant to enlist
psychology to understand his inner life, have been reduced to
wrestling with the same scanty evidence. But it is with his feelings about his mother that they necessarily begin. Elizabeth
Dickens was good-looking, good-natured, youthful beyond her
years, observant of the world around her, competent in managing

her household, more competent in fact than her feckless husband. She taught her eldest son to read and she stimulated his responsive imagination. Not surprisingly, then, the documents that survive—private letters and reports from observers close to the Dickens family—suggest that in return her famous son for the most part treated her with fond, slightly condescending respect.

But one notorious incident undercut his loving sentiments. The jovial and irresponsible John Dickens—Charles Dickens would paint an affectionate portrait of him as Mr. Micawber in *David Copperfield*—could not manage his steadily deteriorating business affairs, and, with his bills unpaid and nothing left to pawn, he ended up in debtor's prison. Grateful to have any income at all, John and Elizabeth Dickens unhesitatingly sent the twelve-year-old Charles to work in a blacking warehouse, pasting labels. He was devastated by his parents' eagerness to subject him to this martyrdom and by the apparent collapse of his ambitious fantasies about the future. There was worse to come. In an autobiographical statement that Dickens wrote in the mid-1840s, first published posthumously in John Forster's biography, he reported that several months later, his father wanted him to stop working and go to school, a move his mother opposed. The fragment records his enduring, unforgiving rage, alive a quarter of a century later: "I never afterwards forgot, I never shall forget, I never can forget, that my mother was warm for my being sent back."

No wonder that students of Dickens have fastened on this sentence, and discovered its echoes in his savage caricatures of unworthy mothers. For them, the most telling example has been Mrs. Nickleby in *Nicholas Nickleby*: snobbish, conceited, naive, full of bad advice, not half as clever as she likes to think. It is hard to know whether this speculation is justified; Dickens was rarely

given to disclosing the real-life sources of his characters. But to
single out this imagined personage and other menaces like them
at the expense of deeper emotional sources for his Esther and his
Agnes is to overlook the sheer complexity of a boy's attitudes
toward his mother. In his ambivalence, more strongly marked, I
believe, than in less sensitive souls, his urge to resurrect the ideal
mother in the figure of young, impeccable beauties must have
been overpowering. He wanted to find ways of remembering his
mother just as David Copperfield liked to remember *his* mother:
young, vivacious, pretty, loving, and (his father fortunately having
died) all his own.

Dickens's odd and lasting love for his sister-in-law, Mary
Hogarth, underscores his need for idealized women in his life.
Mary, one of Catherine Hogarth's younger sisters who spent much
time with her and her new brother-in-law, was by all accounts, not
just Dickens's, a true charmer: very good-looking, full of vitality
and interest in life, intelligent, at ease with that rising literary star,
her brother-in-law, and not at all in love with him. "She had not a
single fault," wrote Dickens, looking back. Then, at seventeen,
showing no sign of illness the day before, she suddenly died, in
his arms. He was devastated: he found himself unable to write,
and postponed a monthly number of the *Pickwick Papers;* he kept
every memento that would remind him of her; he wanted to be
buried in her grave; he dreamed about her night after night for
months, and intermittently for decades after. When, seven years
after Mary Hogarth's death, he happened to meet a young woman
who looked like the girl he had lost, he took a strong interest in
her. Nor did he ever cease thinking about Mary; never worked
through his mourning for her. A strange infatuation that, by definition, was beyond realization, a piece of secular idolatry he could

not give up. Thus, unending mourning begat melancholy, one of Dickens's prevailing moods. Agnes Wickfield was his first attempt to bring her back to life, and Esther Summerson was his second.

DICKENS, THEN, COULD FORM HIS LEADING character in *Bleak House* from deeply felt experiences embroidered by imaginative fantasies. Did he also have a personal stake in his assault on the Court of Chancery? Some literary critics, I know, would call this an illegitimate, because it is an unliterary, question. Still, it remains worth asking because there is no denying that he was making a political point against a governmental institution; indeed, as I have suggested, against all government. It so happens that in 1844, he had been briefly enmeshed in a Chancery suit that frustrated and infuriated him. In January, he sued an unscrupulous publisher who had brazenly plagiarized his *Christmas Carol,* and found a sympathetic hearing in court. "The pirates are beaten flat," he rejoiced on January 18. "They are bruised, bloody, battered, smashed, squelched, and utterly undone." But the pirate declared bankruptcy, dragging Dickens into thorny legal squabbles for which he had no taste, and in May, in disgust, he abandoned the action, having, as he lamented, wasted time, energy, and at least £700.

Hence, when, late in 1846, another plagiarist helped himself to his work, he decided to do nothing about it. "It is better to suffer a great wrong," he wrote to John Forster in a revealing letter, "than to have recourse to the much greater wrong of the law. I shall not easily forget the expense, and anxiety, and the horrible injustice of the *Carol* case, wherein, asserting the plainest right on earth, I was really treated as if I were the robber instead of the robbed." He admitted to "a morbid susceptibility of exasperation, to which the meanness and badness of the law in such a matter would be stinging in the last degree." He was issuing a powerful and comprehensive indictment; for Dickens, the English law was more pernicious than many of the crimes it had been created to punish.

This reluctance to expose himself to irritation and impotence seems reasonable enough. Still, Dickens's responses to these crimes against intellectual property are too fragile a peg on which to hang a long novel. We have seen that he was morbidly sensitive. His boundless literary imagination, which he exploited to the delight of his public, also disposed him to embroider a genuine grievance until it grew into a cause. There is a sizable element of reprisal for injuries suffered—and injuries imagined—in *Bleak House*, as he made the most of his disagreeable experiences. The novel is a lovingly cultivated display of hatred.

5

THE SURVIVAL OF THE MEDIEVAL COURT OF CHANCERY into his times is only one of the charges that Dickens levels against his society in *Bleak House*. With Jo, the pathetic crossing sweep, he takes the novel into the slums of London with its appalling living conditions. That Jo unintentionally infects Esther Summerson with his disease—probably smallpox—is, like the fog, at once a real and a symbolic event. It spreads the horror that is Tom-all-Alone's, Jo's pestiferous district in the metropolis, to respectable society, to people who never walk through its streets, or even acknowledge its existence. "There is not an atom of Tom's slime,"

Dickens writes with more than a touch of *Schadenfreude,* "not a cubic inch of any pestilential gas in which he lives, not one obscenity, not a wickedness, not a brutality of his committing, but shall work its retribution, through every order of society, up to the proudest of the proud and to the highest of the high. Verily, what with tainting, plundering, and spoiling, Tom has his revenge." Dickens's choice of that last word, "revenge," is noteworthy. It is the word of an angry man.

Contemporary reviewers were well aware that Dickens was making a large statement with Jo. The author, wrote one of them, "has never produced anything more rueful, more pitiable, more complete than poor Jo. The dying scene, with its terrible morals and impetuous protest, Mr Dickens has nowhere in all his work excelled." This is more than description, it is resentful diagnosis. In Dickens's hands, Tom-all-Alone's almost consciously tries to get even with a society that permits this sort of misery, with bacilli rather than with riots.

There were too many Jos in Britain, too many Tom-all-Alone's, to let Dickens rest easy. His politics add up to an irate humanitarianism, and it pervaded more and more of his work. Just a few years before, in 1849, Dickens had written a set of three articles on the Tooting baby farm, which show him, the fuming social critic, at the summit of indignation and scorn. During a cholera epidemic of that year, some 150 pauper children had died at Tooting, and the callousness, the sheer inhumanity of the director who let it happen was all too evident. The place had been woefully overcrowded, with the children sleeping four to a bed in foul-smelling, unsanitary rooms, malnourished and largely reduced to eating rotten potatoes, in torn clothes, beaten when they complained, with no medical attention despite a two-weeks' warning that an outbreak of cholera was imminent. "They were half-starved," Dickens wrote, "and more than half-suffocated." The contractor who profitably superintended the establishment was indicted and tried, but escaped punishment when the judge directed a verdict of acquittal on the ground that there was no proof that the child named in the indictment had died as a result of his treatment at the farm.

The scandal and its outcome gave Dickens ample room to raise his sarcasm to heights of bitterness. "Of all similar contractors on earth, Mr. Drouet was the most disinterested, zealous, and unimpeachable." Was he not in charge of a paradise? "The farmed children were slumbering in the lap of peace and plenty; Mr. Drouet, the farmer, was slumbering with an easy conscience, but with one eye perpetually open, to keep watch on the blessings he diffused, and upon the happy infants under his paternal charge." Dickens reported that the publicity the case had secured had pretty well ruined such farming, but that did nothing to abate his righteous wrath against Drouet. But he reserved his most mordant scorn for the authorities that had allowed this catastrophe to occur and then blandly trivialized it after the fact: the local coroner had not bothered with an inquest, the board of guardians had been criminally negligent in their supervision, the presiding judge had browbeaten, insulted, and ridiculed witnesses, and found occasions for facetious remarks much appreciated by the audience.

IT IS ONLY NATURAL THAT DICKENS'S HEATED SATIRE in *Bleak House* should have displeased its victims. His invasion of controversial political issues troubled perhaps as many as it delighted. Enthusiastic readers missed Dickens the humorist, the maker of unpolitical pathos; they wanted him to reproduce his earlier triumphs, the *Pickwick Papers,* which had made him famous, and *David Copperfield,* which had made him England's favorite writer. In these earlier novels he had kept social criticism relatively subdued. But now he was presuming to pronounce on the failings of British society at large, and his massive offensive angered officials enough to have them issue rebuttals.

The Lord Chief Justice, Lord Denman, a loyal reader and his cordial acquaintance, was only the most exalted personage to strike back at Dickens's attacks on his Court. If there were delays in Chancery, he said at a public dinner in the author's presence, they were the responsibility of a nation too parsimonious to give that Court the number of judges it needed. Dickens thought this apologia simply absurd, and said so. For their part, Protestants of the evangelical persuasion were put off by Dickens's heavy mockery in his portrayal of Esther's godmother, whom he had stigmatized for wholly lacking in humor and loosing her gratuitous malice on a helpless child. For the same reason they stoutly objected to Dickens's wicked sketch of Mr. Chadband, that egregious Low Church orator and glutton who gets oral pleasure from hearing himself spout, regurgitates meaningless clichés, and enjoys nothing so much as a free lunch. Lawyers too, so often Dickens's targets, found little to gratify them in a novel that showed them to be vulgar, often sanctimonious exploiters, always prepared with a glib rationalization for their much-maligned profession. Mr. Vholes, Richard's attorney who solemnly guides his client down the road to sure ruin, and who talks interminably of his father and his three daughters for whom he feels responsible, sums up the case for the defense: " 'We are the victims of prejudice.' "

Finally, Dickens has his fun with Mrs. Jellyby, the telescopic philanthropist, who aroused the ire of John Stuart Mill for spite-fully misrepresenting an independent-minded humanitarian woman. "That creature Dickens," Mill wrote to his wife, "whose last story, *Bleak House,* I found accidentally at the London Library the other day and took home to read—much the worst of his things, and the only one of them I altogether dislike—has the vul-gar impudence in this thing to ridicule rights of women. It is done in the very vulgarest way—just the style in which vulgar men used to ridicule 'learned ladies' as neglecting their children and house-hold etc." This was not the way that Mill saw these active, con-science-ridden, often disinterested feminists, and how history has come to see them.

In denouncing Dickens's Mrs. Jellyby, who in her blithe absent-mindedness destroys her husband and criminally neglects her chil-dren for the sake of some presumably needy, remote African tribe, Mill was in a minority as he generally was on the woman question in his day. Most reviewers thought the lady, with her inky fingers and her benevolent, smiling indifference to her so-called loved ones, a delightful creature. But there can be little question that in *Bleak House,* Dickens set out to offend as many constituencies as he could manage; he was an equal-opportunity satirist. His crit-ics belittled his many-pronged campaign as misinformed and self-indulgent, but he had no such compunctions. Self-appointed to set things right, he thought he must be heard.

THIS, AT LEAST, IS HOW DICKENS LIKED TO THINK OF himself. In March 1850, he prefaced the first issue of *Household Words* with an address to his readers. The name of his weekly was to be a sign of its unforced, familiar tone. "We aspire to live in the

Household affections, and to be numbered among the Household thoughts of our readers." The editors, he noted, hoped to "bring into innumerable homes, from the stirring world around us, the knowledge of many social wonders, good and evil," thus to make writers and readers alike ardently persevering, tolerant, faithful in human progress, and "thankful for the privilege of living in the summer-dawn of time." Characteristic of his mind-set, Dickens added: "No mere utilitarian spirit, no iron binding of the mind to grim realities, will give a harsh tone to our *Household Words*, in the bosoms of the young and old, of the well-to-do and the poor, we would tenderly cherish that light of Fancy which is inherent in the human breast."

Here were the planks for a plausible political agenda that a moderately liberal Victorian could endorse. The weekly would frighten no readers with subversive proposals or doctrinaire proclamations. "Oh Heaven for a world without an ism," Dickens had written to a friend in 1844. There would be no propaganda in *Household Words* advocating the leveling of the classes, for that would be dreaded socialism. There would be no Utilitarianism, for that was too materialistic and too calculating to have any appeal to Dickens; it made no place for fancy. When it came to the condition-of-England question, he was in the camp of Thomas Carlyle, its premier expert, to whom Dickens would dedicate *Hard Times*. To be sure, he repeatedly violated his pledge of keeping a harsh tone out of his magazine; but there were simply too many pressing evils to be put into the stocks for all to see.

Walter Bagehot, economist, essayist, editor, and impressive political thinker, once described Dickens's ideology as "sentimental radicalism." True: Dickens was sentimental, but not radical. His heart was for the most part in the right place—for once this

worn formula works, for his political opinions were largely grievances raised to a more general level. They were a matter of com-
passion aroused by some outrageous acts and fed by a highly
cultivated sense of empathy. He took great public controversies
and made them his own, which is why he was better at being a
novelist than a philosopher.

It would be simplistic to say that a shocking event determined
which causes he would champion, but shocking events confirmed
his sense of outrage. Witnessing a hanging helped him to oppose
the death penalty—until in his later years he withdrew from his
abolitionism to favor hanging in the absence of witnesses. Being
victimized in Chancery did not exactly raise his esteem for that
institution. At the same time, he could be harsh and uncompre-
hending toward causes that failed to enlist his sympathy or organ-
izations that irritated him with what he denigrated as their
fanaticism, their excessive claims, their disagreeable, talkative
advocates. "Peace Society, Temperance D[itt]o," he wrote a friend
in the summer of 1851, "who have lately been making stupendous
fools of themselves." That is why he had no use for the sort of
"advances" then being proposed for the handling of prisoners in
Her Majesty's jails. In *David Copperfield,* he had already satirized
coddled "Pet Prisoners," convicts spoiled by unreasonably easy living conditions and delicious food. Had he known more about the
realities of prison life, he might have supported some of the
reforms he mocked.

BUT WHO WOULD DO THE REFORMING OF WHICH
Dickens approved? His novels attest that to his mind the only
desirable and effectual remedies for public ills are private actions

taken by moral individuals, men and women born flawless. They are among his weakest, most irritating inventions. In fact, some of his humanitarians, like the Cheeryble brothers in *Oliver Twist,* with their unfailing smiling goodness, their very name, are hard to take. So, at times, is Mr. Jarndyce; incomparably munificent and disinterested, made all the more admirable (and unbelievable) with his heated protests against being thanked for anything.

Granted, Dickens's novels feature a few characters able to learn from experience, persons who grow to be better than they had been. Invariably, the teacher of these pleasant exceptions in his repertoire is love, pure affection puncturing the masks of reserve, selfishness, and cynicism. Mr. Dombey, in *Dombey and Son,* rises above his cold, irrational aversion for his daughter, Florence, to emerge as a doting father and grandfather. The lovely Bella Wilfer, in *Our Mutual Friend,* overcomes her superciliousness and her mercenary search for a rich husband to love a man for his own sake. David Copperfield educates his heart.

And *Bleak House,* too, features humans who are only human. Mrs. Snagsby, the stationer's jealous wife who suffers a paranoid episode in which she questions her husband's fidelity, is taught by Inspector Bucket (the only character in this novel who enjoyed universal approval among Dickens's readership) to renounce her unreasonable suspicions. We have already noted Sir Leicester Dedlock's late-emerging sterling qualities. But for the most part, the virtuous characters in *Bleak House* are virtuous beyond credibility. Allan Woodcourt is the doctor of every patient's dreams: always available, making house calls day and night, indifferent to money; in a word, worthy of Esther Summerson. And Esther, as we know abundantly by now, is good enough to deserve him.

However dubious these superhumans may seem to us, they

were central to Dickens's strategic intentions. He created the likes of Woodcourt and Jarndyce as a counterpoint to what he deplored as the ludicrousness, the callousness, the sheer viciousness of English institutions. "Inefficiency" would have struck him as far too mild a term to characterize their defects. Infallibly resistant to all change, unable to adapt to new situations or to respond decently to emergencies, they poisoned everything they touched. The brilliantly named "Circumlocution Office" in *Little Dorrit,* a government bureau dedicated to "perceiving—HOW NOT TO DO IT," employs officials like Tite Barnacle (another brilliant piece of naming), perfectly amiable and not openly villainous. But cordial bureaucrats like him work for a government department that has villainy built into it, an invincible contrivance of idleness and corruption.

This was strong stuff. James Fitzjames Stephen, historian, jurist, and judge, an intelligent conservative open to moderate government reform, dryly observed in his review of *Little Dorrit* that Dickens had imagined the Circumlocution Office to demonstrate "that the result of the British constitution, of our boasted freedoms, of parliamentary representation, and of all we possess, is to give us the worst government on the face of the earth—the clatter of a mill grinding no corn, the stroke of an engine drawing no water." This attitude, which Stephen maintained lay at the heart of Dickens's "political novels"—*Bleak House, Little Dorrit, Hard Times*—struck him as wholly unjustified by the evidence, and the notion that the Circumlocution Office was an appropriate metaphor for government in Britain as simply preposterous.

He had a point. In 1851, a year before Dickens published the first installment of *Bleak House,* the Court of Chancery underwent its first significant reforms, even though a few cases rather like *Jarndyce and Jarndyce* were still being heard. It was a brave effort at reorganization to which Dickens's novel gives no space. And it was in 1854, just before Dickens started writing *Little Dorrit*, that the celebrated Northcote-Trevelyan Report proposed a drastic reorganization of the British civil service, including the radical recommendation that positions be filled through competitive examinations. For centuries, ambitious young men had relied on personal connections to enter, and rise in, government service. Some years before, Lord Melbourne, twice prime minister and adviser to the young Queen Victoria, had famously praised the Order of the Garter because, he said, "There is no damned merit in it." Now, in the years that Dickens was sharpening his political pen, the impulse for reform (launched in 1832 by the Great Reform Act, which markedly widened the suffrage) was actually starting to include merit among the conditions necessary for employment in government.

This urgency to make a new, more equitable Britain spread to other fields. Successive Parliaments dramatically cut the list of capital crimes, passed legislation to limit the hours of children working in factories and mines, instituted far-reaching administrative and parliamentary procedures, and began to address the vexed subject of popular education. Not that all was well between classes in Britain; it is arguable that old conflicts between the working and the middle classes grew more acute around midcentury than they had been before. And there was powerful, often effective resistance to reform, even to plainly needed reform, in Parliament and out. Dickens did not fail to notice these maddening obstructions and commented sardonically on them all. In *Household Words*, he deplored the destructive power of Red Tape, Red Tapists, and Tapeworms, and recounted the strange story of Mr. Bull's house-

keeper, Abby Dean—who stands, of course, for the Aberdeen min-
istry of the early 1850s—suffering an unpleasant attack of som-
nambulism. Abby Dean goes about her life while asleep.

All this must remind the reader of the scornful way that Dickens
disposes of cabinet government in *Bleak House*. In a social gath-
ering of high society at the Dedlock mansion, there is much talk
about the current prime minister and the chances of his being
forced to resign. Should he do so, the choice of his successor will
be "between Lord Coodle and Sir Thomas Doodle," always "sup-
posing it to be impossible for the Duke of Foodle to act with
Goodle," and so forth down a stretch of the alphabet. We must
conclude that Dickens's contempt for the Court of Chancery was
exceeded only by his contempt for Parliament.

But in the face of Dickens's failure to appreciate them, the
forces of reform—sanitary reform, factory reform, educational
reform, even parliamentary reform—had the wind in their sails,
all within his lifetime. In 1867, three years before his death, the
Second Reform Act went far beyond its predecessor of 1832 to
enfranchise most males in the country. Yet neither in his novels
nor in his periodicals, except for a few kind words praising Boards
of Health and the like, did Dickens advert to these mitigating circumstances and hopeful signs. The conclusion seems inescapable,
then, that for Dickens, politics was a matter far more of passion
than of information. Nor did consistency much trouble him. One
close reader of Dickens, George H. Ford, has called him an anarchist, and startling though this epithet may seem at first glance,
it is to the point, especially when we specify it more closely by
adding the adjective "angry." For all his protestations to the contrary, Dickens's commitment to the Reality Principle was at best
intermittent.

Dickens's hostility to authority never faltered. And that is why he needed his paragons, his Esthers, his Woodcourts, and his Jarndyces: he never swerved from his conviction that only private decency and charity could ever redeem the dismal English condition. And since their qualities seemed to him all too rare and far from powerful enough, Dickens, the angry anarchist, could not but exaggerate their goodness quite as much as he exaggerated the vices of his all too imperfect country.

HOW, THEN, SHOULD THE STUDENT OF THE PAST READ *Bleak House*? With caution. The work, like Dickens's other late novels, displays an unconquerable distaste for Britain's legal and political institutions, and for its supposed unwillingness to mend what to his mind desperately needed mending. To the extent that this was a mood he shared with liberal and radical reformers, the historian of mid-nineteenth-century Britain may see this novel as a symptom of alienation. But there is little else to commend Dickens as a political thinker. This does not mean that readers should deny themselves the ample pleasures that *Bleak House* has to offer, or refuse it entry into the exclusive club of major novels. It is just that as an aid to the searcher for historical truth, the book urgently calls for second opinions.

TWO

◈

THE PHOBIC ANATOMIST

GUSTAVE FLAUBERT IN

Madame Bovary

"FOR TWO DAYS I HAVE BEEN TRYING TO ENTER INTO *the dreams of young girls* and for this I have been navigating in the milky oceans of literature about castles, troubadours in velvet caps with white feathers." In early March 1852, Flaubert was reporting to Louise Colet, his *"chère Muse"* in these years, sending an early bulletin in what was to become a running commentary on *Madame Bovary*, the novel he had just launched. He was documenting himself conscientiously. "I have just been rereading several children's books for my novel," he wrote, "half crazy" after perusing "old keepsakes" and "tales of shipwrecks and buccaneers." He was serving the Reality Principle, intent on faithfully capturing the debased romantic tastes that would help encompass the ruin of young Emma Rouault, his hapless heroine.

Flaubert remained wedded to his scholarly pursuit of reality throughout his writing life. As soon as he completed *Madame Bovary* in late 1856, he did not rest to celebrate but promptly started on *Salammbô*. This new literary venture, an exotic tale about ancient Carthage blending a love story, a revolt of mercenaries, and barbaric orgies that allowed him to indulge his tastes for erotic violence, first committed him to a course of intensive research. The Romans, we know, had left very little that might testify to posterity about the culture of their North African rival, but Flaubert was undeterred. He inquired about the books on Carthage in the municipal library of Rouen; he perused learned periodicals; he hounded acquaintances for bibliographical information. In May 1857, he found himself "in the midst of reading a quarto-sized 400-page memoir on the pyramidal cypress, because there were cypresses in the courtyard of the temple of Astarte." And by the end of the month he could attest that since March he had read "fifty-three different works on which I have taken notes."

Though he claimed to be suffering from "an indigestion of old books," and confessed that his "formidable archeological labor" frightened him, Flaubert defied his friends' sage council to stop reading and start writing. "Do you know how many volumes about Carthage I have gulped down by now?" he rhetorically asked one of them in July, and answered his own question: "about a hundred." Yet he was adamant about his need for more research. There is a certain note of boasting in these complaints, but a reading of *Salammbô* strongly suggests that he had studied as hard as he claimed. Nor did he find reading enough: in April 1858, he went on a brief excursion to Tunis and Morocco to see for himself— not Car$age, to be sure, but at least the landscape. He needed to feed his imagination with facts.

Flaubert gave his later fictions the same solidity, anchoring them with particulars diligently collected and shrewdly employed. His *Education sentimentale* takes its provincial anti-hero Frédéric Moreau to Paris at midcentury, and returns to him, middle-aged, in 1867, to his not very mature maturity. Moreau's most intensely explored experience is the revolution of 1848: the disorder in the

streets, the Utopian schemes of socialist idealists, the radical political clubs with their interminable debates that sprang up after King
Louis Philippe abdicated in February. In writing these impressive,
if rather sour pages, Flaubert, who had been in Paris during the
early months of the revolution, used his memory. But not that
alone. He importuned one friend to send him reminiscences of
club life in those heady months, and another to explain how one
could make and lose a fortune on the stock market in short order
during these years. He read the pamphlets of the Utopian social-
ists and back numbers of newspapers for the year 1848.

To lend one of his scenes the kind of authenticity he wanted,
he even spent several hours at the Hôpital Sainte-Eugénie in Paris
watching children suffering from the croup, a harrowing experience. "It was abominable," he told his beloved niece Caroline, "and
I left there heartbroken. But art above everything!" He enjoyed
being thought "too truthful." As for himself, his fictions could never
be truthful enough.

Certainly neither the performers in *Madame Bovary* nor their
performances crossed the boundaries of ordinary human nature.
Loosely based on a true episode, it tells the story of the handsome,
moody daughter of a prosperous Norman farmer (thoroughly bourgeois in his outlook) who marries an *officier de santé,* a health officer without a medical degree. He adores his wife but he, in turn,
bores her. After a time of mounting disillusionment, she indulges
her pitiful luxuriant fantasies, takes in succession two lovers who
callously exploit her gullibility and her unfulfilled erotic needs,
plunges into debt to buy lavish presents for these roués, falls into
the hands of a pitiless local usurer, and, seeing no way out, com-
mits suicide. Nothing unrealistic about any of it.

Not even Emma Bovary's most egregious transgressions, her

adulteries, strain the reader's credulity. In his appreciative review of *Madame Bovary*, Baudelaire flatly called adultery "the tritest, the most prostituted human situation, the most broken-down barrel organ of all." Surely it was a familiar enough device for novelists. Even Dickens, prudent Dickens, provocatively toyed with this theme. We recall Mrs. Snagsby, in *Bleak House,* under the temporary (wholly unjustified) delusion that her husband is having an affair. And in some of his other novels, Dickens slyly aroused his readers' suspicions that adultery has been or is about to be committed, only to draw back. In *David Copperfield,* Annie Strong, the young, beautiful wife of the elderly scholar Dr. Strong, convincingly rehabilitates herself from the charge that she has been carrying on with her dashing cousin; in *Dombey and Son,* Edith Dombey, Mr. Dombey's wife, raised to be an expensive, heartless object for sale to the highest bidder, retains enough moral strength to refuse herself to her would-be seducer, the villainous Mr. Carker. But other novelists rushed in where Dickens feared to tread. Nathaniel Hawthorne's *The Scarlet Letter,* Leo Tolstoy's *Anna Karenina,* Theodor Fontane's *Effi Briest,* Henry James's *The Golden Bowl,* are only the most prominent tales of adultery in nineteenth-century fiction. *Madame Bovary,* then, was working a rich, almost inexhaustible vein of all too human fallibility.

The issue of adultery had particular relevance to Flaubert's France. In 1816, the year after the Bourbons returned to the French throne, they repealed the divorce legislation passed during the Revolution, and divorce was not restored until 1884—four years after Flaubert's death. Under these circumstances, breaking the marriage vows was a plausible, perhaps necessary recourse for a restless husband or a neglected wife. Hence in *Pot-bouille,* a volume in his *Rougon-Macquart* cycle, Zola depicts the Parisian bour-

geoisie from high to low avidly engaged in the sport of illicit, extramarital love; the most timid of wives, he intimates, will fall into
infidelity from ignorance, boredom, the lust for pleasure, and sheer
passivity in the presence of a confident and determined worldling.
Allowing for dramatic overstatement, we may read this novel as
working within the compass of probability in a country without the
safety valve of divorce. In 1883, as new divorce legislation was being
bitterly debated across the country, Zola noted, only half facetiously,
that if the proposed law passed, it would be the end of French literature. What on earth would novelists write about? Emma
Bovary's adventures with Rodolphe, her first, and Léon, her second lover, then, were fairly common, almost expected, even in the
provincial backwater where *Madame Bovary* largely takes place.

FLAUBERT'S UNRELENTING SEARCH FOR TRUTH IN
fiction went beyond mundane details in his characters' inner lives.
He was, of course, not the first novelist to explore the minds of
his creations. But Flaubert did so with unexampled intensity. His
most memorable pronouncement about his work is doubtless
"Madame Bovary, c'est moi." Students of his oeuvre have rightly
read this exclamation as a terse testimonial to his highly developed gift for entering the most secret precincts of his characters.
But beyond that, it was also part of his passion for truth pushed
to new limits.

One might think that Flaubert rejoiced in this talent. In fact,
he suffered under it. In 1852, he told Louise Colet: "Last
Wednesday I had to get up and fetch my handkerchief. Tears were
running down my face. I had been moved by my own writing."
Years after completing *Madame Bovary,* he told the eminent liter-

ary and political historian Hippolyte Taine that when he had done
the scene near the end in which Emma Bovary takes poison, he
had gone through two attacks of indigestion, could not rid himself of the taste of arsenic in his mouth, and vomited up his dinner. An author's identification with his creations cannot be closer
this side insanity.

His father, the physician Achille-Cléophas Flaubert, director of
a hospital at Rouen, had indirectly warned him of the havoc that
undue preoccupation with a powerful theme may produce. "My
father always said that he should never have wanted to be a physician in an insane asylum," he wrote Louise Colet in 1853, "because
if one works seriously with madness, one ends up catching it." This
did not stop the son. Two decades after finishing *Madame Bovary*,
he once again burrowed into his characters so deeply that he could
no longer keep them and himself apart. It was in the mid-1870s,
when he was slaving over his sarcastic (and, as usual, most meticulously prepared) analysis of two petty bourgeois, that he wrote:
"*Bouvard* and *Pécuchet* fill me up to such a point that I have
become them! Their stupidity has become mine, and I am bursting with it."

But this technique of exploring his characters by living *in* as
much as *with* them, all the more effective no doubt for being not
just conscious, stood in productive tension with a determination to
keep distance from his creations, to establish his authorial sover-
eignty with "scientific" impersonality. He wanted to be objective
about subjectivity. In a thoughtful early review of *Madame Bovary*,
Charles-Augustin Sainte-Beuve, France's most influential literary
critic and the author's friend, introduced an apt metaphor that others did not fail to copy: "Son and brother of eminent surgeons,
Monsieur Flaubert handles the pen as others do the scalpel.

Anatomists and physiologists, I find you on every hand." In a well-known caricature which looks like an illustration to Sainte-Beuve's figure of speech, J. Lemot depicted Flaubert in a surgeon's apron, holding in his left hand a scalpel with Emma Bovary's heart skewered on it, dripping blood, and in his right an outsized magnifying glass. Part of her body appears to the rear at left. Such medical allusions could only gratify him; he thought of his style as a dissecting instrument. To use it was one way, a favorite way, of expressing his splenetic worldview.

Obviously, the interplay of a writer's mind with his literary creations is never simple. Flaubert was aware of that. "It is a strange thing," he wrote Louise Colet, "the relation between one's writings and one's personality." It was even stranger, even more complicated, than he thought. One reason for this complexity is Flaubert's emotional link to, and distance from, the romantics. On the surface, one may read *Madame Bovary* as a manifesto against romanticism. It is a commonplace petty bourgeois tragedy—so commonplace in fact in its characters and its protagonist's fatal flaw that the novel scarcely deserves so lofty a label. The evidence for the incurable mediocrity of Emma's mind and of the local gentry who surround her is beyond question—in all not the kind of fiction that a romantic would have written.

But within the framework of Flaubert's dominating preoccupations, *Madame Bovary* is, if it is a manifesto, one directed only against romanticism debased. We may reasonably understand the novel as a defense of *pure* romanticism, of which Flaubert shows his invented characters—and implicitly most of his fellow novelists—to be incapable. Certainly the statement, "*Madame Bovary, c'est moi*," is a star witness for Flaubert's informal affinity with the romantic clan. An assertion of the most passionate individuality, this identification proclaims a profound intimacy between creator and creation that a neoclassicist could never have cultivated. The exotic "romantic" topics on which Flaubert would expend years of labor—ancient Carthage and the temptations of Saint Anthony—attest to the same disposition. Nor did he ever disavow the romantic spirit at its best. In 1857, thanking Charles Baudelaire for sending him a copy of *Les fleurs du mal,* he told the poet that with his originality, his uniqueness, he had "found the way of rejuvenating romanticism." Full of admiration, he added, "You resemble no one, (which is the first of all qualities)." He knew no higher praise.

Hence, when adversaries of the romantic camp made themselves heard, he assailed them with all the resources of his scatology-drenched vocabulary. In 1865, after reading Proudhon's *Du principe de l'art,* which paid tribute to Courbet's Realist canvases, he sarcastically exclaimed: "All for Courbet's glory and for the demolition of romanticism!" The book reminded him of having to get to a latrine walking on turds every step of the way. Earlier, in May 1857, thanking Sainte-Beuve for his review of *Madame Bovary,* he had described himself as "an impassioned, or if you will, crusty, old romantic." In later years, returning to self-definitions, he said so again more than once, and called himself a romantic fossil—unique, much like Baudelaire. He saw himself, in short, as a special brand of romantic with a passion for reality.

FOR ALL HIS LOYALTY TO THE REALITY PRINCIPLE, IT DID not occupy the summit of Flaubert's pantheon. That was reserved for Art or, as he sometimes put it, for style, with Truth occupying an honored second place. "The morality of Art," he wrote in December 1856, "consists in its very beauty, and I value it above all else, first style and then Truth." These two ideals were for him not rivals but partners. Art needed Truth, and Truth served Art. The sentence from a letter to his niece Caroline that I have quoted before—"but art above everything!"—is revealing in this context, for, we will recall, Flaubert inserts this accolade into a description of his doing some traumatic empirical research. He was, by his lights, above all a poet, a truthful poet. *"Je suis né lyrique."* That is why he almost always capitalized the word "Art." Serving these eternal ideals, he showed himself, as he confessed himself to be, a good Platonist. No wonder that as a humble worshiper in the temple of Art, he did not much care for Zola's naturalism: it lacked poetry.

Flaubert used the vocabulary of religion when he spoke of Art, but his was a highly idiosyncratic kind of irreligious religiosity. He saw himself, he informed Louise Colet, as a priest, the guardian, in other words, of an exclusive coterie of civilized literary men and women. This creed made him severe with philistine remarks even when his lover uttered them. In January 1847, he vehemently criticized her "singular" suggestion that someone write a continuation of Voltaire's *Candide.* "Is that possible?" he put her in her place. "Who will do it? Who could do it? There are works so dreadfully great (this is one of them), that they would crush anyone who tried to bear their weight. Giant's armor: the dwarf who put it on his back would be flattened before taking a step." He thought that there was something fundamentally wrong in her aesthetic judgment. "You have a genuine love of art, but not its religion." This was not a stricture he would ever need to apply to himself. With all its imprecision, even its occasional self-contradictions, his idea of Art was virtually sacred to him—and nothing else. In April 1853, he laid it down to Colet: "a thinker (and what is an artist if not a triple thinker?) ought to have neither religion, country, not even any social convictions." No commitment could have been more categorical.

Wrestling with style as he hibernated in his study at Croisset working long hours gave Flaubert exquisite pain but even more exquisite pleasure. Not that he slighted the demands of his body; it was partly for its sake that he would make the trip from his home near Rouen to Paris to spend a night with Louise Colet. "I love my work with a love that is frantic and perverted," he told her in April 1852, hardly giving *her* exquisite pleasure with this confession, "as an ascetic loves the hair shirt that scratches his belly." And he fiercely proclaimed, underlining the sentence in his ardor: *"The artist must elevate everything!"* Not since Shelley had called the poet the unacknowledged legislator of the world had any imaginative writer made such exalted claims for the vocation of letters. "The artist must be in his work like God in his Creation invisible and omnipotent, whom one senses everywhere but does not see."

This high-flying pronouncement was more than a profession of his animating faith, it was also a plea for his stylistic principle of keeping the omniscient narrator as much out of sight as possible. His extravagant rhetoric had a certain reality for him: there *was* something divine about writers—well, a few writers. To Flaubert, reverence for Art meant reverence for a small pantheon of dazzling practitioners. He was known for being a good hater, but he was capable of admiration no less. Among his contemporaries he singled out Baudelaire, Tolstoy, Turgenev, George Sand, and Victor Hugo—the last of these with strong reservations. And he often dreamed of having lived in better times, when people really believed in Art—ancient Athens, Rome, or the Renaissance.* "It seems to me," he told Louise Colet, "that if I were to meet Shakespeare, I would burst with fear." He would have been just as tongue-tied with Homer, Virgil, Rabelais, Cervantes, Voltaire, Goethe.

BETTER TIMES, WHEN PEOPLE BELIEVED IN ART! IT was plain to Flaubert that he was doomed to live in despicable times. His letters, early and late, abounded in snide references to French culture when he was a schoolboy, and as a seasoned novelist he did not revise his opinion. He hated what he called in 1855, in a letter to his intimate friend, Louis Bouilhet, his "rotten century! And we are stuck," he added, "in first-rate shit!" Nor did he see much room for improvement. "I deny the literary renaissance you proclaim," he wrote to Maxime du Camp in July 1852. "So far, I see no new writer, no original book, no idea that is not stale." A year later, he told Louise Colet that he found his culture almost unbearable. "The hatred I see everywhere directed against poetry, against pure Art, the complete denial of the True gives me an appetite for suicide." When a more cheerful mood was upon him, which was rare, he would grant that a less dispiriting future was not unthinkable—but not in his lifetime. "The time for beauty is over," he wrote to his muse in April 1852. "Mankind may return to it, but it has no use for it at present."

The collective villain who had brought French literature to this

---

*"I have reread Michelet's *Roman History*," he wrote to his friend Maxime du Camp in 1846. "Antiquity gives me vertigo. Surely I have lived in Rome in the times of Caesar or Nero.—Have you sometimes thought of an evening of triumph, when the legions returned, when the perfumes were burning around the conqueror's chariot and the captive kings marched behind, and afterwards this old arena? Look, that's where one should be living." G.F. to Maxime du Camp (May 1846). *Correspondance*, I, 266.

pass was, to Flaubert's jaundiced mind, the bourgeoisie. It roused
his considerable gift for abuse to its highest pitch. Nor were fellow writers immune from his poisoned arrows. "What makes me
indignant is the *bourgeoisisme* of our colleagues! What merchants!
What dull imbeciles!" If we can trust his splenetic outbursts, bourgeois—their looks, their clothes, their speech, their opinions—
quite literally made him sick. In October 1872 (to give a ripe
instance), his good friend, the novelist and critic Théophile
Gautier, died at sixty-one. He had been suffocated, Flaubert persuaded himself, by an excessive exposure to modern stupidity: *la
bêtise moderne*. A few days later, he ran into three or four bourgeois
in the streets of Rouen. "The spectacle of their vulgarity," he
exploded to his niece Caroline, "their frock coats, their hats, what
they said and the sound of their voices, made me want to vomit
and to cry at the same time. Never since I have been in this world
have I been choked by such disgust." Doubtless he overstated the
intensity of his nausea; he had often recorded such queasiness
before. A few days later, he told his friend, the playwright Ernest
Feydeau, that he wished it were himself rather than Gautier who
was rotting in the ground. "But before perishing, or rather, while
waiting to perish, I want to 'void' the gall that fills me. Hence I am
preparing to vomit. It will be copious and bitter, I promise you."

This unmeasured distaste for the middle class never rose to the
level of reasonable social criticism; Flaubert included the lower
orders in his global condemnation. "I use the word 'bourgeois,' "
he told George Sand in 1871, "to include *messieurs* the working
people." He had defined the term in the same inclusive, and soci-
ologically useless, way before—often. They were all, whether
wearing frock coats or overalls, dim-witted and in all probability
doomed to remain so.

THE TEXT OF *MADAME BOVARY* SEEMS DESIGNED TO support this verdict. It serves to prove that bourgeois could love as little as they could do anything else really well. In fact, it is the failure in this elemental passion that triggers the evolution of the plot. Much to Emma's dismay, her sex life with her husband was perfunctory, almost mechanical. "His transports," Flaubert writes, "had become standardized; he embraced her only at certain hours. It had become a habit among others, and like a predictable dessert after the monotony of dinner." Domestic reality, especially in bed, was anything but the romantic stories she had swallowed as a girl.

As I noted at the beginning, Flaubert spent untold hours on Emma Rouault's reading matter. Jimmy Walker, New York's flamboyant mayor during the 1920s, once said, "No girl has ever been seduced by a book." Emma was an exception to this sweeping assertion. She was seduced by a book, or, better, by many books. At the age of thirteen, she had been sent to a convent run by kindly nuns, and it was there that her awakening sexual imagination found ample supplies of new images, new feelings. Her devotions never rose above their carnal embodiments. What fired her up was the "mystical languor exhaled by the perfumes of the altar, the coolness of the holy water fonts, and the radiance of the tapers."

In short, the faith the nuns preached and so devoutly practiced presented itself to Emma in pictures in which lust hovered just beneath the surface. Her religious enthusiasms, Flaubert notes, always lingered on what she could see, smell, hear, and touch. She loved the church for its flowers, the music for its dreamy words, and the literature for the passionate excitement it could stir up. That is why "when she went to confession she invented small sins that she might hang back as long as possible on her knees in the shadows, her hands joined, her face at the grille, beneath the priest whispering." The metaphors repeatedly used in sermons— "betrothed, spouse, celestial lover, eternal marriage—thrilled her with unexpected sweetness to the bottom of her soul." There was something childlike about her impatient physicality: "She had to extract a sort of personal profit from things," Flaubert sums it up, "and she rejected as useless everything that did not contribute to her heart's immediate pleasure—being of a temperament more sentimental than artistic, looking for emotions and not scenery."

Emma's reading only reinforced her habit of translating her religious instruction into sensual delights. During her stay at the convent, she avidly consumed novels. Chateaubriand's romantic melancholy had spoken to her, though his worship of nature left her untouched; she knew the world of the farmyard too intimately to find it a source of excitement. In contrast, Sir Walter Scott's novels, on which she tumbled not long after, fed her choicer morsels. And not content with squeezing erotic images from the classics of her day—it is at this point that Flaubert's researches into the dreams of young girls paid off—Emma swallowed sentimental songs, inane love poems, and trashy tales about aristocratic lovers and swooning maidens, beautiful ladies and noble gentlemen, audacious rescues and thrilling embraces. "She would have liked to live in some old manor like those chatelaines in long bodices, who, under the trefoil of ogive arches, would spend their hours, elbows on the stone and chin in hand, and watch a white-plumed knight galloping on a black horse from the distant open country."

In time, the fantasies that Emma Bovary's orgies of reading nourished made her married life ever harder to endure. After her wedding, she had persuaded herself "that she at last possessed that marvelous passion that had so far been like a great bird with rosy plumage hovering in the splendor of poetic skies,—and now she could not believe that the tranquility in which she lived was the happiness of which she had dreamed." If she had read less, she would have suffered less.

FLAUBERT ONCE SAID THAT HE WANTED TO WRITE A BOOK about nothing. *Madame Bovary* was not that book, for it was a weapon in his arsenal for a lifelong campaign against stupidity, greed, philistinism. His nausea and phobic response to what he was pleased to call the bourgeoisie require an exploration of his character. Without detracting from the genius of a writer who gave world literature one of its imperishable monuments, we must track down the emotional demons with which he wrestled, for that should serve to define his relation to reality, to his book and his culture. It was Flaubert, after all, who invented Emma Bovary and Salammbô, Frédéric and Rosanette, and the rest of his imagined worlds.

Flaubert's vengeful diatribes far surpassed any objective grounds for grievances against middle-class society. He suggested that he and his friends, sitting on his balcony, watch the public go by and spit on their heads. He hoped that *Salammbô* would "annoy the bourgeois, that is to say, everybody." He claimed that he would like nothing better than to burn down Rouen and Paris. He wanted to throw the revolutionaries of 1871 into the Seine. We cannot minimize such heartfelt desires as merely a failed effort at manly humor. Flaubert's oppressive repetitiousness lends a certain psychological weight to these manifestations of an acerbic temper. In some measure, his hatreds were symptoms: his phobia was like all phobias a defense against anxiety, less troubling than the terror against which it was designed to insulate the sufferer. The phobic's inhibitions, whether he cannot cross a bridge or watch a bourgeois without breaking out in a sweat, are his armor. Yet such protective stratagems are bound to fail: Flaubert's fits of choking and vomiting, even if less severe in reality than in his reports, were signs that he could not keep his anxiety at bay. Becoming like Emma Bovary or like Pécuchet was more than a helpful strategy to make literature. For him, the son and brother of bourgeois, it was his worst nightmare, and with that perhaps his deepest wish.

There are two tactics for dealing with phobias, and Flaubert resorted to them both. One was to isolate himself as much as he could from the philistines, lest contact with them contaminate him. His festive dinners in Paris with like-minded literary friends were acts of self-protective sociability, since they were never sullied by the presence of a good bourgeois. The other was to adopt the counterphobic attitude, to face the cause of his revulsions head-on. His unremitting concentration on his "uncultivated" fellow citizens, industriously collecting their sayings, documenting their attitudes, and ceaselessly anatomizing their conduct, were valiant acts of confronting the enemy.

Flaubert, then, was a writer in conflict, unsettled even about the remedies that might serve him best. And his inner sparring points to what the celebrated French neurologist Jean-Martin Charcot once called, in Freud's hearing, *la chose génitale*, that most potent of all causes. Certainly, for Flaubert, the genital thing was a lifelong predicament. He never resolved his inconsistent feelings about the place of sexuality in his life, uncertain whether to embrace or to flee his temptations. For one thing, Eros had a persuasive competitor: his work. From the start of his affair with Louise Colet, he was stirred again and again by the urge to be alone. Though eleven years older than he and an experienced occupant of some illustrious beds, she had maintained her not inconsiderable beauty. Yet he would tell her, often and rudely, that for him love must always yield to the demands of Art. "For me, love is not and must not be in the foreground of life. It must remain in the back of the shop." Intent on keeping himself separate from his *chère Muse*, he urged her to love Art rather than him. When in 1843 the sculptor James Pradier had advised him to start an affair, Flaubert demurred. "I have reflected on Pradier's advice," he informed Alfred LePoittevin, an intimate of his youth, "and it's good. But how to follow it?" Pradier's wife, an attractive young woman liberal with her favors and separated from her husband, was briefly his mistress at the time, which, especially the "briefly," suited him. He admitted that an affair "is what I need, still it's not what I will do. Normal, regular, well-sustained and stable coitus would take me too much out of myself, would disturb me. I should re-enter active life, into physical reality, in fact common sense, and that has harmed me every time I have attempted it."

Hence, to gratify his appetites and to keep his private space as uncluttered as possible, he occasionally went to a whorehouse. In some tactless letters to Louise Colet, he praised the oldest profession and claimed to find it fascinating. The thought of marriage terrified him and so did the prospect of fatherhood. When Colet intimated that she might be pregnant, he begged her to have an abortion. It pleased him that she lived in Paris, a comfortable distance—comfortable for him. Still, Flaubert wanted her, for a variety of purposes. His letters to her are a remarkable mixture of erotic reminiscences ("You cried out, 'Bite me, bite me!' Do you remember?"), brilliant little essays on writing, and professions of literary faith. When he got away from France during an eighteenth-month voyage to Egypt and the Near East in 1849 and 1850, he made the trip one long orgy (which included handsome boys for hire). He copulated with, among many others, a celebrated courtesan, Kuchuk Hanem, making fierce love, or at least reporting it back home to his intimates—though not to his mother—in long letters, giving crass details ("I sucked her furiously") and much lascivious word painting.

FLAUBERT'S EROTIC EPISTOLARY PROSE, RATHER toned down in his published writings, suggests the persistence of unfinished childhood business. In his novels, he played with Oedipal themes, with parricide and its converse, the killing of a disloyal son by his pitiless father, and with a dangerous blending of maternal and sensual love. In real life, he had some trouble keeping the two apart. Byron, he once wrote significantly, adored Italy as one would a mother or a mistress. His intimacy with his younger sister, Caroline, who had been his companion in youthful theatricals and his confidante all her short life, has a curiously subversive, far from subtle erotic aroma ("What kisses I send you!" she wrote to him when she was eighteen and he twenty-one). As with other humans, his thoughts went where his actions did not follow, but he did write them down. Typically, as a lapsed Catholic, his irreverence was extreme, almost programmatic. He fantasized about having sex in an Italian church: "It would be pleasant to fuck there in the evening, hidden behind the confessionals at the hours when one lights the lamps." He once noted, before he had published anything, that he wanted to write a story about a man's love for an inaccessible woman that would make the reader tremble with fear. He knew, and he said, that there were some desires he dared not touch, notably his sister—and Elisa Schlésinger.

For he did fall seriously in love once and, to judge from his writings, remained faithful—in his way. Another rumored love, Juliet Herbert, the English governess of his niece Caroline, seems, in the absence of almost all evidence, largely a charming possibility. The passion about which there *is* evidence was for Madame Schlésinger, the wife of a genial, astute, rather unscrupulous businessman. When Flaubert met her, on the beach at Trouville, he was fifteen and she twenty-six—precisely the difference in age that would separate him from Louise Colet. Elisa Schlésinger was tall, dark, voluptuously built, somewhat languid—and unavailable because she was faithful to her philandering husband.

He never touched and he never forgot her. An early autobiographical story, *Mémoires d'un fou*, tells how he fell in love with her. "Maria," as he calls her, "had a child, a little girl; she was loved, she was embraced, she was wearied with caresses and kisses." How he wished he could have "gathered up a single one of these kisses." Maria "nursed her herself, and one day I saw her uncover her bosom and give her child the breast." This had really happened at Trouville, and the sight seems to have remained with him. "It was a fleshy and round bosom, with brown skin and azure veins one could see under that ardent flesh. I had never seen a naked woman before. Oh! The singular ecstasy into which the sight of that breast plunged me, how I devoured it with my eyes, how I would have liked just to touch it!" He had a fantasy of biting it passionately, "and my heart dissolved with delight in thinking of the voluptuous pleasures that this kiss would give me."

More than three decades later, in *L'Education sentimentale*

(1869), Elisa makes a prominent appearance, half mother figure for Frédéric and half longed-for mistress, the unattainable woman of his dreams. Three years after that, in a touching letter of apology to Elisa, Flaubert excused himself for not writing sooner, and a little pathetically gave fatigue as the reason. "The more my life advances, the sadder it is. I am returning to complete solitude. I send best wishes for your son's happiness as though he were mine and I embrace both the one and the other— but you a little bit more, my ever beloved—*ma toujours aimée.*" She was a full-flown bourgeoise, but in her case Flaubert was willing to make an exception.

CONSIDERING HIS EXPERIENCES AS AN UNRECONSTRUCTED bachelor, fanatic of style, and professional outsider up to the publication of *Madame Bovary*, Flaubert could not have been astonished if in 1857 respectable Frenchmen denounced him for pandering to the lowest human instincts. They were—weren't they?—only acting in character. In the novel, the most arresting representative of middle-class conceit and idiocy was Monsieur Homais, the local apothecary, with his irrepressible commonplaces, thoughtless mouthing of progressive formulas—Homais is a *Voltairien*—and unshakable self-importance. One scene in which he stars is particularly telling. Homais is lecturing his young clerk for committing a possibly fatal mistake in filling a prescription. As he shakes the clerk in anger, a book drops from the boy's pocket; it is called *Conjugal Love* and, to make it more alluring still, it has illustrations. When Madame Homais steps forward

to get a glimpse of this interesting publication, her husband impe-
riously waves her away. "No!" he yells. "Don't touch it!" No doubt
Homais would have forbidden his wife to read *Madame Bovary.*.

It was only to be expected that in Flaubert's other fiction,
unsatisfactory lovers like Charles Bovary should reappear. In
L'Education sentimentale, Frédéric Moreau has mistresses in
Paris, but his true love escapes him (just as did Flaubert's). The
novel concludes with one of most emphatic anti-sentimental end-
ings in modern literature: Frédéric reminisces with an old friend,
singling out the time many years ago when the two had presented
themselves at the door of a local bordello only to turn back in
panic. That, they agree, was the best time they ever had!

And those lower-middle-class rentiers, Bouvard and Pécuchet,
are even less lucky in love. Having inherited some money, they
move awkwardly, amateurishly, across the spectrum of learning—
agronomy, geology, medicine, philosophy, theology—only to suffer shipwreck in each attempt to educate themselves. In passing,
they utter the bromides that Flaubert had been collecting for
decades. When, in their frantic quest for encyclopedic wisdom,
they turn to investigate sexual love, they are humiliated once
again. Bouvard is rejected by an avaricious widow, Pécuchet
catches a venereal disease from their maid. In short, Charles
Bovary, with his well-intentioned, clumsy, utterly prosaic lovemaking, sets the standard for respectable sexuality as Flaubert
assessed it.

In startling contrast to these amorous underachievers, Emma
Bovary's lovers were more than merely competent, but neither
acquits himself as a good bourgeois. Rodolphe, a landowner of
thirty-four, "had a brutal temperament and a shrewd intelligence.
Having had much to do with women, he knew them very well."

There would be more of them once he had finished with this delicious morsel that had virtually fallen into his lap. While he was
working out his strategic moves to entrap Emma Bovary, that pre-
maturely jaded housewife both pretty and inexperienced, he was
already beginning to calculate just how to get rid of her after he
had tired of her, as he surely would. This was a routine with him
before he had even possessed the mistress of the moment. But
with Emma Bovary, boredom seized him more slowly than he had
expected. As his liaison prospered and she fell ever more under
his sinister domination, he perceived, Flaubert notes, "that in this
love affair he could exploit other sexual gratifications. He decided
that all restraints were inconvenient and treated her rudely. He
made her into something pliant and corrupt." In his sketches for
the novel, Flaubert put it more plainly: Rodolphe treated Emma
like a whore, he "f——d her to death."* Yet not wholly against her
will. She loved him all the more for his roughness with her. "Hers,"
Flaubert comments, "was a sort of idiotic attachment filled with
admiration for him and voluptuousness for her." She loved him,
Flaubert said in his notes, like a god. Emma Bovary, in short, did
Rodolphe's work for him.

She did quite as much for Léon, the law clerk with whom she

---

*Highly skilled at drawing a veil over details of sexual couplings, letting the reader
do the work of filling out the scene, Flaubert does not specify just how Rodolphe
corrupts Emma Bovary during lovemaking. No doubt quite unaware of the erotic
implications of the gesture, implications that have become commonplace since
the advent of psychoanalysis, he describes Emma after intercourse in his château:
"she would explore the set of rooms, she would open the drawers, she would
comb her hair with his comb and look at herself in the shaving mirror. Often she
would even put between her teeth the stem of a large pipe which was on the
night table amidst the lemons and lumps of sugar near a carafe of water" (441
[II, 9]). It is a charming still life—charming and laden with sexual possibilities.
But sometimes, of course, a pipe is just a pipe.

had been infatuated for his sentimental speeches before he went off to Paris to further his legal education. There he had learned much about life from the grisettes, only to return a wiser but scarcely a better man. "His shyness," Flaubert observes, "had worn off after his contacts with lively company, and he had returned to the provinces despising everyone who did not tread the asphalt of the boulevards with feet dressed in patent-leather." This gave him a considerable advantage over his provincial mistress and he used it.

▣ IN THE MINDS OF MIDCENTURY READERS, THE ISSUE OF sexuality in *Madame Bovary* was paramount, more disturbing even than its questionable piety. In a substantial and searching review of the novel in 1857, James Fitzjames Stephen—we have met him before, going after Dickens—judged it to be packed with indecencies, and its heroine "disgusting." He noted that it had "excited great attention at Paris, and has been hailed with much applause, as a specimen of 'realism' in fiction, by very eminent critics."* Stephen failed to recognize Flaubert's supreme ambition: not to be typecast as a member of any school, but rather to be first and last himself. If he admitted to being in any company at all, it would be, as we have seen, a select, self-identified elite.

Stephen insinuated that *Madame Bovary* was the sort of novel only to be expected from French writers. This is one way in which Flaubert's readers allow his masterpiece to expand its relevance to larger issues, to questions of national styles in candor and ret-

---

*We recall from the Prologue (see p. 18) that Flaubert did not appreciate this tribute. "People believe that I am smitten with the real, while I execrate it, for it is in hatred of realism that I have undertaken this novel."

icence. For, despite all his reservations, Stephen recommended the novel to a limited audience. It was worth the attention "of all who take an interest in the condition of French society." From small to large: Stephen greeted the book as a witness to—perhaps better, as a symptom of—the morals of a whole culture.

Yet he misjudged the reception of the novel in France. For there were Frenchmen—and Frenchwomen—who found *Madame Bovary* as offensive as any prudish Englishman or American ever did. In 1856, when the novel was running serially in the *Revue de Paris*, edited by Flaubert's politic and inconstant friend Maxime du Camp, angry voices called for its suppression. Du Camp was uncomfortably aware that his magazine was under the baleful eye of the censors for its liberal views. He had been warned more than once that one of these days the authorities might shut it down. And so, in December, he refused to print that memorable scene which details, without a single exceptionable word, the mad, meandering ride in a *fiacre* through Rouen in which Emma and Léon make love all day. Even though he recognized the reason for du Camp's prudence, this act of self-censorship infuriated Flaubert. He wanted the text he had so patiently and painfully dragged out of himself kept intact at all costs.

Events confirmed du Camp's uneasiness. In January 1857, almost as though to prove his prescience, the state put the author, publisher, and printer of *Madame Bovary* on trial for obscenity and blasphemy. The decision to proceed with the case mystified Flaubert, and it has never been quite cleared up. Almost until that day, he thought that his access to prominent personages would keep him safe from prosecution. In December, he had still been lighthearted, rather enjoying his spreading notoriety. "The *Bovary* is progressing above my expectations," he wrote. "People find that

I am being too truthful." Then, when it looked as though he might actually be put into the dock, he explained this as the government's subterfuge to make him a scapegoat. "I am a pretext. They want to demolish the *Revue de Paris.*" The whole affair, he wrote to his brother, Achille, was a "political matter." But by mid-January, he thought the true explanation even more devious than that. He speculated that the *Revue* was itself only a pretext. "There is behind all this *something*, something invisible and tenacious." One did not need to be a devotee of conspiracy theories to sniff hidden machinations in the background.

Flaubert's unresolved puzzlement documents that midcentury France was a deeply divided society. More than half a century after the Revolution, the French were still debating its nature and its consequences. And that debate continued to be exceptionally fierce because the historic event launched in 1789 had not been the last upheaval to agitate the country; political instability became a regular feature in French life. In 1815, following upon the hectic years of Napoleon I, the Restoration brought the Bourbon dynasty back to the throne and frantically tried to revive the supposed glories of the Old Régime. But this anachronism was annulled in 1830 with a bloodless revolution, as the Orléanist wing of French royalty took office, and with that (most contemporary observers believed) the upper bourgeoisie. It lasted just eighteen years, overthrown in 1848 and replaced by the short-lived Second Republic. But this radical experiment (increasingly less radical with the passing months) enjoyed an even shorter life: on December 2, 1851, Louis Napoleon, Napoleon I's nephew, who as president had sworn to uphold the republic, usurped power in a coup d'état, and precisely a year later had himself crowned Napoleon III.

It was not a solution that Flaubert welcomed, but like most other French men of letters, he grudgingly submitted to the new realities. Victor Hugo, the most notable exception, scornfully called the new emperor *"Napoléon le petit,"* an attitude Flaubert shared and expressed—in private. How else could he feel about a regime that severely censored dramas, newspapers, even poets? Not long after the trial of Flaubert, it would be Baudelaire's turn to be put in the dock, for *Les fleurs du mal*, poems that, the judges found, with their obscene and blasphemous realism, unduly excited the reader's senses. The consequence: a fine of 300 francs and the exclusion of certain verses in any next edition. Open eroticism was forbidden; the string of mistresses that the emperor permitted himself were, of course, another matter. "Weren't people freer and more intelligent in the times of Pericles than in the times of Napoleon III?" Flaubert asked Louise Colet in 1854. He did not wholly make peace with the empire—no regime, perhaps, apart from a dictatorship led by men of letters, would have suited him, for Flaubert, much like Dickens, was an anarchist at heart. But at first, when *Madame Bovary* was being threatened with prosecution, he thought he would be spared.

The Empire of the Nephew had put an end to open political discontent, but it did not heal the deep splits in French society. Those who remembered the French Revolution with authentic nostalgia were indifferent, even hostile, to Roman Catholicism; believers, probably a majority especially in the countryside, feared the anti-clericalism among the working class and liberal professionals as a danger to the spiritual health of their country. Napoleon III, the English historian Alfred Cobban has tersely observed, "never became more than an adventurer, even when he was on a throne." There were certain accomplishments to which he could point: the expansion of the railroad system, the ambitious modernization of Paris. But there was always something unsavory about his regime, which the glitter of Jacques Offenbach's witty and tuneful operettas could not wholly conceal.

A devious man, the emperor had shrewdly reached an accommodation with the church and secured the support of well-disposed, respectable Frenchmen. Hence most historians have seen the affair of *Madame Bovary* as Flaubert eventually came to see it: as a political matter. The state prosecutor, Ernest Pinard, must have been put up to it by higher authorities! Or was he an opportunist assiduously shoring up a highly promising career, simply taking it for granted that action in the name of Christianity and good morals was what his superiors wanted? Surely, a public display of religious vigilance would not be amiss.

As I have suggested before, sometimes a cigar, even a noble Havana, is just a cigar. The truth about this prosecution may have been fairly simple. There are times when the lesson of Edgar Allan Poe in "The Purloined Letter" applies to motives: the apparently most hidden is actually the most visible. To judge from the energy with which he conducted the prosecution, it seems that Pinard had been shocked by *Madame Bovary*, partly won over by its literary power, partly convinced that he must protect the public from such tempters to immorality. He was so driven by his mission that when his superiors tried to take him off the case, he strenuously protested. The book was a cause he had made his own. "Who will read M. Flaubert's novel?" he gravely asked the court. "Is it men occupied with political or social economy? No! The flighty pages of *Madame Bovary* will fall into the hands of even flightier ones, into the hands of young girls, sometimes into those of married women." That late in life

Pinard would publish a book of obscene poetry, a delicious irony that did not escape Flaubert, in no way discredits his zeal as a young prosecutor. It only underscores the familiar truth that in course of their lives, human beings are often the playthings of incompatible needs.

In his address to the court, Pinard applauded Flaubert's artistry but condemned his licentiousness. Quoting what he stigmatized as immoral and sacrilegious passages from the novel— two seduction scenes, Emma Bovary's briefly recovered religiosity between her two affairs, and her last moments—he concluded that the author had employed all the resources of art without any of its restraints. "He uses no gauze, no veils, it is nature in all its nudity, in all its crudity." And at least three times he directed the court's attention to what he called the "poetry of adultery." But the defense attorney, Marie A. J. Sénard, was more than a match for his adversary. He utilized the author's valuable assistance in picking out steamy paragraphs from recognized French classics and from Montesquieu, the unimpeachable representative of the French Enlightenment. When he came to the charge of blasphemy in Emma Bovary's death scene, Sénard pointed out that the author had borrowed the Roman Catholic ritual used at such solemn occasions, translated it into French, and toned it down. He won the day. Flaubert and his fellow defendants were acquitted. Their only punishment: having to listen to a harangue from the bench for failing to write and publish an edifying book.

The trial proved an exhausting and frightening business, more so than Flaubert could admit. In the end, it did not change him or his views: far from being the cause of his indictment of the French bourgeoisie, it only confirmed it. After all, he had been a bourgeoisophobe for some twenty years by then. But he did take comfort in shows of support from influential circles. "Ladies," society women with impressive connections, he noted, became *"Bovarystes enragées."* Some even appealed to Empress Eugénie to spare their favorite author the anguish of a trial. Not all his support was wholly welcome. Fitzjames Stephen came to the unacceptable conclusion—certainly unacceptable to Flaubert—that he had intended "to write rather a moral book," what with the sinful heroine's excruciating demise.

In France, meanwhile, Flaubert found some unexpected allies. Alphonse de Lamartine, statesman, major poet and minor historian, claimed to know *Madame Bovary* by heart and volunteered to intercede. Even if in 1857, facing a capricious regime, Flaubert needed all the help he could mobilize, he must have found this particular champion embarrassing, because he thought little of Lamartine as a novelist. Some five years earlier, writing to Louise Colet, he had called Lamartine's latest novel, *Graziella*, the best thing he had done in prose, but nonetheless mediocre. He had failed even to hint at sexual passion. "To start with, to speak plainly," he grumbled about Lamartine's handling of the protagonists' love, "does he sleep with her or does he not sleep with her? These aren't human beings but mannequins," and so, "the principal thing is so surrounded by mystery that one doesn't know what to think—sexual union being systematically relegated to the shadows, like drinking, eating, pissing, etc." Flaubert was not likely to be guilty of such prudery—witness *Madame Bovary.*

THIS, OF COURSE, HAD BEEN PINARD'S POINT ALL along: the pervasive mood of the novel was sensuality unleashed; the quotations he had selected, he told the court, were far from

doing it justice. He was right: had he wanted to convey the eroticism that pervades the book like a pungent perfume, he would
have had to recite it all. Even as a young girl, Emma had given
hints of erotic delirium to come. Charles Bovary, not particularly
sensitive as a rule, was instantly attracted to her. He had visited
her family farm to set her father's leg and, once he had a good
glimpse of Emma, he came back—to see her rather than his
patient, who was recovering nicely. In a scene drenched in inti-
mations of erotic thrills to come, Flaubert exhibits Emma as half-
aware of herself as a temptress. It is a memorable passage.
Accompanying her visitor on his departure from the farm, Emma
would stand with him to wait for his horse. "One time, a day of
thaw, the bark on the trees in the courtyard was oozing sap, the
snow on the roofs was melting. She was on the doorstep, went in
to look for her parasol and opened it. The parasol, of shot silk,
with the sun pouring through it, lit up the white skin of her face
with mobile reflections. She smiled beneath it at the mild
warmth, and could hear drops of water falling, one by one, on the
taut watered silk." The scene reads like a scenario for Monet
painting his Camille in the bright outdoors. Even Charles Bovary
finds himself vaguely aroused by the drumming of those drops on
Emma's parasol and the beads of sweat on her bare shoulders in
the sun.

Emma is an earthy being. She chews on her lips as she listens
silently, and when she pricks her finger with her needle, she sucks
it in a suggestive, though wholly unconscious gesture. One day, as
Charles Bovary comes to see her, she offers him a companionable
glass of curaçao, fills his little glass to the brim, and pours a few
ceremonial drops for herself. After touching glasses with him, she
raises hers to her mouth. "Since it was almost empty," Flaubert

records the moment, "she threw herself back to drink, and, her head bent back, her lips pushed forward, her neck stretched, she laughed at tasting nothing, while the tip of her tongue emerged between her fine teeth and licked the bottom of the glass with little thrusts." This reads like a carefully planted vignette to foreshadow a very similar posture in Emma's future, during a far guiltier encounter.

For there will come another time when Emma, now Emma Bovary, bends back, this time at a turning point in her life. Rodolphe subjects her to his will at last, after a long day's effort at persuasion, outdoors. "The cloth of her riding habit caught on the velvet of his coat, she leaned back her white throat which swelled in a sigh, and trembling, all tears, with a long shudder and hiding her face, she gave herself to him—*elle s'abandonna.*" Times have changed: we no longer find this passivity acceptable; it makes woman the captive who surrenders to the triumphant sexual conqueror. But Flaubert's language reflects his time and accurately captures her frame of mind, part anticipation, part shame, as she averts her face at the critical instant.

That shudder will reappear in an encounter with Léon. They quarrel repeatedly and make up, but she finds each of their couplings yet one more letdown. In a despairing search to rekindle Léon's affections, she throws herself at him with greater abandon than before. "She constantly promised herself profound happiness at the next encounter; afterwards she acknowledged to herself that she had felt nothing extraordinary. That disappointment quickly faded under new hopes, and Emma returned to him more excited, more avid. She undressed brutally: she tore at her thin corset laces, which hissed around her hips like a gliding snake. She would tiptoe on her bare feet to see once more if the door was locked; then, in a single gesture she let fall all her clothes;—and, pale, silent, grave, she would collapse on his chest, with a long shudder."

Pale, silent, grave, shuddering: Flaubert misses few opportunities to remind his readers that Emma Bovary's extramarital escapades give her more misery than joy. True, she enjoys a certain honeymoon time with Rodolphe and, later, with Léon; after she has first slept with Rodolphe, she feels exuberant: "I have a lover!" she says to herself. "I have a lover!" But she is haunted by anxiety that she may lose what she has so brazenly acquired and is so expensively keeping. There are times, indeed, as she pursues her reckless, mad assignations, when she wonders whether it might not have been better if she had remained a good, faithful Madame Bovary. As she has to find ever more extravagant, ever riskier excuses to meet her lovers, her desire for sexual gratification is so intimately mingled with rage that she finds it impossible to separate the two.* And, as her affairs come to an end, she will suffer more. Rodolphe, promising to go away with her, deserts her. Léon, when her debts become oppressive, refuses to help her. When, upbraiding Rodolphe for his cynicism, she speaks about the anger of love, she is confessing her true state of mind. Sadly, in her adultery, Flaubert notes, she rediscovered "all the platitudes of marriage."

---

*Once Flaubert shows Emma Bovary disaffected with her boring, bourgeois marriage, he begins to comment, repeatedly, on her furious state of mind—against her husband, against herself, against some unspecified grievances—at the very time her neighbors praise the young wife for her housekeeping. Two instances: "She was filled with covetousness, with rage, with hatred" (389 [II, 5]). And, a little later, after she has fallen in love with Léon: "her carnal appetites, her yearning for money, her melancholy brought on by her passion [for Léon], all merged into one single anguish" (ibid.).

FLAUBERT'S ACCOUNT OF EMMA BOVARY'S READING, HER infatuations, her neighbors' ruthlessness when her money troubles become unmanageable, may at times seem somewhat heavy-handed. But his very hyperbole links his novel to his culture. Like all wielders of satire, he was aware that a measure of overstatement is its lifeblood—though not beyond the bounds of probability! "The means of reaching the ideal," he observed to Hippolyte Taine, "is to write realistically, and one can write realistically only by choosing and exaggerating." But this did not mean that Flaubert ever admitted that the sometimes inspired, always excessive insults he heaped on bourgeois were in any way overstated, let alone unjust. They were, to him, compressed statements about appalling truths that characterized middle-class nineteenth-century French culture.

His society, he believed, was irreparably scarred by a betrayal of self that has been called "inauthenticity" since the mid-nineteenth century. The high ideals that bourgeois professed to esteem were to his mind a farrago of lies, especially lies they told themselves. Marriage, business, politics, religion, the education of children, and the consumption of art, literature, drama, and music were all practiced with an eye to public approval and opportunities for social climbing. Sincerity was the bourgeoisie's first casualty. Whatever epithets critics could throw at the middle class—"hypocrite," "philistine," "swindler," "charlatan," "robber baron," perhaps "grocer" the most potent of them all, at least in France—all of life attested to their accuracy. Bourgeois critics, bourgeois patrons, bourgeois collectors, bourgeois editors were, Flaubert

believed, reigning supreme, and the wreckage they had left behind
was all too evident. At times the bourgeoisie's real taste asserted
itself: the trashy fiction that sent Emma Bovary into ecstasies and
shaped her expectations had long been the favorite fodder of
French readers.

Emma, then, stood as an instructive instance of the general
inauthenticity, a small replica of her society at large. Her narcissism mirrored the narcissism of her neighbors; her behavior was
a poor imitation of her literary models. Not even her sexual adven-
turism was wholly her own; she supply adapted her erotic desires
to the men whose playthings she allowed herself to become.
Rodolphe especially taught her what her "natural" cravings were.
If she had lived today and consulted a social worker, she would
have been told that she was suffering from low self-esteem.

WHETHER HE WAS ASSAILING FRENCH CULTURE WITH
his individualized portrayal of Emma Bovary or his stinging gen-
eralizations, Flaubert's aversion to his world was all-encompass-
ing. He punctuated his letters with the bellicose word "revenge."
In 1853, identifying himself with Louis Bouilhet's low spirits over
his uncertain literary fortunes—*Louis Bouilhet, c'est moi!*—he
advised him to treat society as harshly as it has treated him and
loyally took his grievance personally: "Oh! I'll avenge myself! I'll
avenge myself!" Much like Dickens, Flaubert carried grudges
against any handy target—really against all society. When, two
years later, the Théâtre Français rejected a drama of Bouilhet's,
he comforted his friend in the same tone: "The obstacles you are
encountering confirm my ideas. All doors would open if you were
a mediocre man." Bouilhet's naïveté astonished him: "So you don't

know that in this charming country of France, they execrate originality!" and he vented his spleen with characteristic coarseness: "I feel against the stupidity of my epoch waves of hatred that choke me. Shit mounts to my mouth, as in strangulated hernias." As he told George Sand in 1867, "To dissect is to take revenge," and to dissect, we know, was what he did best.

In a discerning review of *Madame Bovary*, Baudelaire sensed its fundamental motive to be a kind of willed contrariness. He saw its author making a statement of implacable discontent, as he worked off his revulsion against his country by exploring the most unpromising subject imaginable—precisely because it was so unpromising. "On a banal canvas, we shall paint in a style that is vigorous, picturesque, subtle, and exact," he imagined Flaubert thinking. "We shall put the most burning and passionate feelings into the most commonplace adventures. The most solemn utterances will come from the most imbecile mouths. What is the very home of imbecility, the most stupid society, most productive of absurdities, most abounding in intolerant fools? The provinces. Which of its inhabitants are the most insufferable? The common people, incessantly engaged in petty employments, the very exercise of which distorts their ideas." This is a subtle intuition, reaching down to Flaubert's ultimate intentions translated into art by force of will and sheer genius.

SURELY IN THE CANON OF MODERN LITERATURE—I AM assuming that there is still such a thing—the prominent, even leading place of *Madame Bovary* remains secure. The novel remains as fresh, as absorbing today as it was a century and a half ago. But its uses to the historian *as* historian are severely limited. As I have shown in some detail, for all its commitment to the Reality Principle, it was not a disinterested presentation of the evidence. Even its innocuous-sounding subtitle, *"moeurs de province—* provincial ways," held a hidden sting, at least for the initiated: those in Flaubert's circle took *"province"* as a synonym for dreariness, conventionality, shallow (or worse, sincere) piety. The book is a weapon of harassment. It tells us more, however determined we may be to learn from *Madame Bovary,* about the predicaments of the French avant-garde, or its author's anxieties, than about the France of Napoleon III, or about Rouen, his birthplace.

After all, in the 1850s, the Norman city of Rouen, whose citizens so nauseated Flaubert, was a port of 100,000 inhabitants that was, admittedly, no mecca of the arts. It was not until 1880, the year of his death, that it opened an art museum. For the writer whose favorite play was *Hamlet* and favorite opera *Don Giovanni,* the Rouennais might not have provided the most fascinating company. But his caricature of them, and of their provincial cousins, as unfailingly crude, avaricious, materialistic, practically interchangeable, did them a considerable injustice. As the capital of its *département*, it was a lively hub of trade and industry, and home to high-ranking government and ecclesiastical officials. It boasted among its richest citizens François Depeaux, shipbuilder, cotton trader, philanthropist, amateur yachtsman, and collector of Impressionist paintings, which were in those years still little regarded. There is good evidence that local bourgeois were readers of high-level fiction, the kind of reading of which Flaubert would have approved, had he taken the trouble to ask them about the novels on their night tables. Some of them even read Flaubert. The notorious definitions in his *Dictionnaire des idées reçues,* which gathered together what he despised as the sum of bourgeois wisdom—"CONCERT. Well-bred pastime," or "NOVELS. Corrupt the masses"—were by no means typical of all Rouennais.

But Flaubert's wish to offend and frighten the straitlaced public won out over his passion for facts. "Will I shock the *others* with it?" he asked in October 1856, as *Madame Bovary* was appearing serially, and answered his own question: "Let's hope so!" Indeed, he could not even resist taking a final jab at respectable France in the last sentences of the novel. After Emma's death, her husband's possessions are sold off to pay the debts she had incurred, and Charles Bovary, overwhelmed by the revelations of his wife's secret life and inconsolable at her death, soon dies of unknown causes—the autopsy revealed nothing—really of a broken heart, a "vaporous flood of love" alive in him to the end. Meanwhile Monsieur Homais, that master of the liberal cliché, has risen to particular distinction in his little town. "The authorities humor him and public opinion supports him. He has just been given the cross of the Legion of Honor." Flaubert wanted to make it perfectly plain: whoever lost, the bourgeoisie won.

THREE

THE MUTINOUS PATRICIAN

THOMAS MANN IN

Buddenbrooks

1

UNLIKE CHARLES DICKENS AND GUSTAVE FLAUBERT, WHO aimed to write aesthetically creditable works of literature, enjoying the discharge of political aggressiveness along the way, Thomas Mann tried for profundity, a quality that has long troubled critics of the German psyche. In his correspondence, autobiographical statements, and interviews that he seems to have greatly enjoyed, he would firmly maintain that *Buddenbrooks,* his first novel, published in 1901 when he was twenty-six, was a deeply German, an "eminently nordic" book. It was, he would say, a moralist's novel and he proclaimed Richard Wagner, "the Mightiest," as his master. Wagner had taught him the uses of leitmotifs and emblematic formulas, "the metaphysical, the symbolic elevation of the moment."

Nor was Wagner his only model; he traced his intellectual heritage also to Schopenhauer and Nietzsche, philosophers rather than novelists. This is to say nothing about his celebrated irony, which he was beginning to make his distinctive signature. Yet not all his readers followed him into the higher realms of thought. "Wide circles," he said a little bitterly, appreciated him mainly as the "recorder of good dinners"; it disappointed him that so many had missed his ambitious program, the conquest of the transcendental.

Yet Mann integrated leitmotifs and symbols into his text so thoroughly that *Buddenbrooks* reads like one of those solid, earthy family narratives then so highly favored. He had formed his characters, he said, "in part from living persons," from "memories of home, dignified and scurrilous," and from "individuals and circumstances that had made an impression on my receptive youth."* The news, he wrote to a friend in 1903, that there "are in my hometown some people who find my life and my aspirations not wholly contemptible is dear to me and valuable. At bottom, one cannot be wholly indifferent to a city about which one writes a book eleven hundred pages long." In short: *Buddenbrooks* was in its author's eyes a book about Lübeck by a novelist born and raised in Lübeck. When the drama critic Julius Bab asked him where Thomas Buddenbrook, the central character, had lived, Mann replied as though he were handing out a real address: "In actuality, Thomas B's house was not in the Fischergrube but in the Beckergrube, which runs parallel to it. It was Number 52." He sounds precisely like the most conventional of Realists, though a Realist who would not be imprisoned by the Reality Principle.

The unrivaled family chronicle in German literature in the last two centuries, Mann's novel traces the rising and decaying fortunes of four generations of a prosperous, civic-minded clan of merchants from the mid-1830s to around 1880, with far stronger emphasis on its downward rather than its upward career. The Buddenbrooks are patricians with strong local pride and ingrained

*"I worked with the help of family papers and commercial information," he wrote to Joseph Warner Angell on November 5, 1937, "which I obtained from my hometown." *Thomas Mann. Teil*, I, 97.

familial self-satisfaction, and the book ranges from Johann Buddenbrook the elder, who consolidated the clan's fortunes, to its last protagonist, Hanno, the end of the family line.

There is a terrifying moment in *Buddenbrooks* when little Hanno, then eight, comes upon the family record in which previous generations have inscribed the most significant days in their lives and occasionally added short comments. He casually leafs through the pages and spots his own names—Justus, Johann, Kaspar, and the date of his birth. Then, just as casually, he takes a ruler and a gold pen and draws two neat parallel lines under the whole. That evening his father, Thomas Buddenbrook, who heads the house in the third generation, happens to notice his son's blasphemy and, in a fury, insists on being told why he has done such a horrible thing. "What is this! Answer!" he snaps at the boy. "I thought . . . I thought . . . ," the frightened Hanno stammers, "there would be nothing more." Thomas Mann was not the writer to invent symbolic moments only to waste them. We know that there will be nothing more.

The setting of *Buddenbrooks* is an unnamed North German town. In the course of following the passing years, the novel traverses all the major markers of family life, courtships, weddings, christenings, birthdays, anniversaries, quarrels, divorces, visits to the dentist. But Mann, fully aware that he was anatomizing a commercial dynasty, did not neglect the way the Buddenbrooks made, and sometimes lost, money. He not only painstakingly registered their manners, tastes, and language—the French phrases that punctuate the speech of the first generation, the patrician mode of addressing servants—but also their doings as businessmen. The Buddenbrooks are merchants of the old school, gentlemen of their word, conservative players in a rapidly changing market place.

They find it all the more galling to have one of their sons-in-law end up a bankrupt, and another, an embezzler, in prison.

Just once one of them, Thomas Buddenbrook, resorts to an unscrupulous maneuver. Hesitantly, after an agonized inner debate, he decides that he will for once set aside the family's principles, which are also his own. He buys up at fire sale prices a large farm owned by an aristocrat desperately in need of money, expecting to sell the harvest at an unconscionable profit. The plea that persuades him to desert rectitude is a reminder by his sister, Tony (who happens to be the struggling Junker's wife's closest friend), that if he fails to take advantage of this bargain, thus generously helping an acquaintance and bringing some new money into the family firm, its rival, the Hagenströms, will jump at it.

It is not greed, then, that sways Thomas Buddenbrook from his honorable habits, but the anxious wish to prove to himself that the Hagenströms have not yet usurped the Buddenbrooks' foremost place in town. Later in the fall of that year, while the firm is celebrating its centennial with pomp and speeches, one of Thomas's underlings brings him a telegram: the harvest has been ruined by a hailstorm. It looks like providential retribution, though the hand of vengeance, of course, and the choice of the utterly fitting time of its delivery, are those of Thomas Mann. It is the metaphysical moralist at work, who could rarely resist creating a spectacular climax. The message is plain: when a Buddenbrook tries to be a ruthless up-to-date capitalist, he will fail even more badly than he will if he never manages to adapt his business strategies to harsher times.

The Hagenströms are symptomatic of these times, a new breed of capitalist, without tradition, without piety for their ancestors, as free to spend money as to make it. The current head of the family, Hermann Hagenström, is genial but, it seems, not overly scrupulous. Mann clearly means the reader to dislike him, since he portrays him as so hideously fat that his double chin has spread, so to speak, to his cheeks. No character in Dickens ever boasted such repulsive bulk. He is a man who has built himself an opulent house that owes nothing to the time-honored architecture of which his fellow citizens are so proud, a man who eats pâté de foie gras for breakfast—in short, the very exemplar of the parvenu. In the end he will take over the once dominant economic position that the Buddenbrooks had once enjoyed and—symbol of symbols!—buy their mansion.

These struggles for economic and social power look like material that the social and cultural historian can only welcome. But Mann insisted that pitting the declining *Bürgertum* against the rising bourgeoisie was never his main concern. Rather, the problem that had stimulated his productivity, he wrote some years later, was a biological-psychological one, a fascination with the human soul. "The sociological-political," he wrote, "I just sort of took along half unconsciously; it concerned me very little." Still, it concerned him enough that when, a few years later, sociologists like Max Weber, Ernst Troeltsch, and Werner Sombart—Germans all of them—wrote treatises characterizing the modern capitalist as a driven, self-abnegating figure, he took care to note that he had already described the type in his novel without any help from social scientists.* Which leaves the question whether Mann, half con-

---

*"I set great store by the statement that I intuited and invented the thought that modern-capitalistic acquisitive man, the bourgeois with his ascetic idea of professional duty, is a creature of the Protestant ethic, of Puritanism and Calvinism, completely on my own, without reading, through direct insight and discovered only afterwards, only recently, that it had been thought and expressed at the same time by learned thinkers." *Betrachtungen eines Unpolitischen, Werke,* XII, 145.

sciously, had perhaps managed to tell the observant historian more about the "sociological-political" domain of nineteenth-century society than he knew he was revealing.

◈ BY HIS OWN TESTIMONY, THEN, MANN WAS AFTER bigger game than writing a "mere" realistic family narrative. What he called the "biological-psychological" that interested him above all was the great matter of life and death. Especially death: until he was about fifty—one can date the end of this infatuation pretty precisely to the early 1920s—he carried on a romantic love affair with death, fed by his three masters, but principally by Wagner. He made the fateful conjunction of love and death—the *Liebestod*—his own. It was only to be expected that he acknowledged *Tristan und Isolde* as a favorite text.

That attitude continued to dominate Mann's mind for years beyond the publication of *Buddenbrooks*. Shortly after completing that novel, he wrote a novella, *Tristan,* that gave his mocking and morbid spirit ample room for display. It takes place in a sanatorium complete with a grotesque "lover" as Tristan, an ineffectual but voluble aesthete, and a young mother as Isolde, a competent pianist whom the physicians have forbidden to play lest the strain worsen her already severe condition—an allusion to the fate of Antonia in Jacques Offenbach's *Tales of Hoffmann* rather than to that of Isolde in Wagner's *Tristan und Isolde*. But like Wagner's heroine, Mann's heroine too will die, not of love but of tuberculosis. In writing *Tristan,* Mann obviously still had Wagner on his mind, yet he could take a certain ironic distance from the master: he calls his story a burlesque. Yet, his astonishing freedom in treating this deadly serious music humorously cannot obscure his deeply pessimistic vision of life, in which Eros implies, and invites, Thanatos.

Tristan and Isolde die apparently longing for extinction, but their deaths are at the same time an expression of brimming vitality. Tristan would appear to be manufacturing obstacles to keep him from consummating his passion for Isolde. But the couple is animated by the fantasy of a bliss indefinitely prolonged. Their fate embodies a philosophy of love articulated in the Victorian decades by such religious poets as Coventry Patmore and Charles Kingsley— neither of them a Wagnerian. For them the promise of paradise was nothing less than sexual intercourse prolonged into eternity. And few professional commentators and plain listeners alike have failed to notice that Wagner's score for the *Liebestod* is voluptuousness incarnate. With its lush orchestration, its swelling cadences, its climaxes, and its peaceful detumescence, it is intercourse set to music.

Nor is it a secret that the fantasy of dying together echoes the consummation of simultaneous orgasm. What the French call the "little death" in carnal embrace wipes out for a climactic moment the boundaries that separate lovers, transcends their individual selves to merge them, most beautifully and most intensely, as they drift into lassitude pervaded by the wish to die this way again, and often. One need not be a Wagner to compose such music; little Hanno, as we shall see, composed a fair approximation to the musical love-death even though his acquaintance with the Mightiest must have been sparse at best.

The burlesque *Tristan* did not sate Mann's appetite for ironic forays into Wagner territory. In 1905, he wrote a short story, "Blood of the Wälsungs," which few have read: he withdrew it from publication, had it printed in a luxurious edition, and never included it in his collected stories. The embarrassing rumor that it was an anti-Semitic tale—the protagonists, inseparable nineteen-year-old twins named Siegmund and Sieglinde, are from a wealthy Jewish family, the Aarenholds in Berlin—would have been especially troubling for Mann after 1933, and he kept it out of general circulation. Sieglinde is engaged to a boring gentile businessman whom she likes far less than she likes her brother. She and Siegmund attend a performance of *Die Walküre,* which brings out into the open what has been implicit all along: their incestuous love for one another. They act it out afterward, at home, in Siegmund's luxurious room, on his bearskin rug. Thus Mann has life imitate art.

THE CONSERVATIVE, NATIONALISTIC POLITICS THAT Mann professed in these early years played into that curious amalgam of eroticism and metaphysical musings he called philosophizing. He insisted that only a German could have written *Buddenbrooks.* In *Reflections of an Unpolitical Man,* that enormous patriotic pamphlet on which he labored through World War I to oppose his older brother Heinrich's cosmopolitanism, he went far enough to ask rhetorically, "Can one be a philosopher without being German?" To be German meant to be deep, to reject as trivial the rationalism so popular in contemporary France and Britain, and as shallow its ancestor, the Western Enlightenment. To the young Thomas Mann, and to many fellow Germans, the philosophes were a traditionless, irresponsible crowd of coffeehouse wits who championed such heresies as human perfectibility, the triumph of prose over poetry, and other naive and blasphemous imaginings. With so solemn a perspective on the world, it was easy to conclude that the end of life—not just its conclusion but its purpose—was death.

These were not impersonal, purely theoretical ruminations for Thomas Mann. During those years he often thought of death, including his own. In early 1901, he disclosed his suicidal moods to his brother Heinrich, to whom he was then, and would be for many years, bound in love-hate tension; he reported "depressions of a really terrible sort with completely seriously intended plans for self-disposal—*Selbstabschaffungsplänen.*" It was a particularly tense time for him; he was anxiously awaiting word from his publisher, Samuel Fischer, whether he would be obliged to make sizable cuts in the vast manuscript of *Buddenbrooks.* Putting a brave face on his situation with forced lightheartedness, he explained to his brother what his novel was really about: "The whole thing is metaphysics, music, and adolescent eroticism."

It is a fair summary of the novel; all three themes duly appear in it. But it is plain that Mann, the Wagnerian troubadour of death, dwelt with particular satisfaction on fatal illnesses. His unstinting descriptions of these royal roads to extinction are among the most admired passages in German fiction; they rival in sheer pitilessness Flaubert's account of Emma Bovary's demise. The contrast to Dickens's moralizing death scenes, with faces turned up to heaven and prayerful resolutions, could not be more pronounced. Thomas Buddenbrook, a respected senator and merchant who gradually loses his taste for business and begins to wonder, in unhealthy ruminations, about the nature of life—especially *his* life—is one of the most spectacular casualties in the book. On his way home from a painful session with his dentist, he suffers a stroke in the street and collapses. There they find him, lying on his face in the muck, his fur coat and his white kid gloves bespattered with filth and watery snow. He will die not long after.

Thomas's only child, Hanno, the last of the clan, will fare no

better. Dreamy and delicate, plainly unfit for business, he loves to
play and fantasize on the piano—though Mann, ever afraid of
being caught in sentimentality, insists that the boy's musical talent is at best a modest one. After reporting at some length on a
typical school day for Hanno (authoritarian and unrewarding) and,
after that, at home—he is now fifteen—Mann abruptly opens the
next chapter in a radically altered, clinical tone: "With typhoid,
things proceed as follows." After two pages of medical description,
it is clear that Hanno must die.

MANN IS JUST AS UNSPARING WITH LESS MOMENTOUS
but still disagreeable topics. He renders, in fulsome detail, the
rather disgusting dinner conversation of Christian Buddenbrook,
Thomas's brother, with its self-pitying and preposterous recitals of
his physical symptoms. No one, in short, could accuse Thomas
Mann of false gentility. In tune with other uninhibited literary
Realists of the time, he did not avert his eyes from the physical
domains of life. Yet there is one elemental theme on which he
touches barely, or only indirectly: erotic love.

In this reserve, Thomas Mann was far closer to Dickens than
to Flaubert, and in tune with other German Realists. The Germans
had come to Realism late, but by the time Mann wrote his first
stories, in the 1890s, they had done much to catch up with their
colleagues abroad. Certain progressive periodicals championed
plays and novels explicit on social issues—the social criticism that
is so prominent a feature in the drama of Ibsen and the novels of
Zola, and so natural an element in all Realism, was becoming more
and more familiar to German writers, as playwrights like Gerhart
Hauptmann and novelists like Theodor Fontane amply attest. But

this candor did not extend to sexual passion, not yet. Flaubert freely describes his heroine indulge in erotic fantasies and how she undresses in haste to join her lover Léon in bed in some shabby hotel. Not so Mann.

In more than a quarter of a million words, a few friendly or familial salutes apart, there are only six kisses in the novel. All but two of them bear significantly on the life of Tony Buddenbrook, who, as the family saga proceeds, begins to occupy an ever more central place. She has appeared in the opening scene as an eight-year-old, being catechized by her mother and grandmother, and she is present at the end, as she, the boy's mother, and assorted mourners talk about Hanno. Earnest, a little snobbish, not overly intelligent but supremely resilient, Tony, though much tried by life, is the great survivor in the family.

The four kisses of which she is the dubious beneficiary or horrified witness do not lead to any happy resolution; they are embarrassed and embarrassing. The first takes place while she is still a schoolgirl, the target of a futile amorous assault by a boy in her class, an awkward pubertal eruption both unclean and unwelcome. Later, as a young woman, she finds her luck improving for a brief time, in an unexpected, spontaneous, unforgettable amorous interlude, the most romantic—the single romantic—moment in *Buddenbrooks*. A Herr Bendix Grünlich from Hamburg, a respectful, even servile businessman with whom her father had had some dealings, seems intent on marrying Tony and has approached her parents to advance his suit. But she energetically refuses to hear of the match because she cordially dislikes Grünlich. Given a temporary respite, she is allowed to flee to a sea resort where she meets Morten, an attractive, idealistic medical student. Their walks and their conversations are all quite inno-

cent and he is quite unsuitable—without his degree!—as a husband to a Buddenbrook.

But one day, as they are sitting together on the beach, she
makes her feelings for him plain and he asks her to seal her promise to love him and not to have anything to do with folk like
Grünlich. "She did not answer, she did not even look at him: she
only slid her upper body on the sand hill a little closer to him,
very gently, and Morten kissed her slowly and awkwardly on the
mouth. Then they looked off in different directions on the sand,
and were ashamed beyond all bounds." She will never see Morten
again, but he will live on in her conversation through the years,
invisibly pitted, much to their disadvantage, against the men she
will marry.

The third kiss is the formal mark of her betrothal to the impossible Grünlich; her father, who has had business reverses, expects
his son-in-law to help recoup his fortunes. "No unnecessary ceremony! No social encumbrance! No tactless caresses! A discreet
breath of a kiss on her forehead in the presence of the parents had
sealed the engagement." Unfortunately, Grünlich, far from being
able to assist the Buddenbrook firm, will be unmasked as a
swindler who confesses that he had married Tony only for her
money. Nor is the fourth kiss any more charming. She has married again, a Herr Permaneder, a hearty Bavarian. He is not a
greedy man—a welcome relief after Grünlich—but given to looking where, as a bourgeois husband, he ought not to look. To her
noisy dismay, Tony catches him wrestling with the maid in an
undignified embrace. She will hear no excuses and refuses all talk
of reconciliation. Thus ends her second marriage.

And the fifth and sixth kisses? In a modest, out-of-the-way
flower shop. Thomas Buddenbrook bestows them on a "wonder-

fully pretty," exotic-looking saleswoman, Anna, who has been his mistress for some time. He is saying farewell to her: to pursue the commercial training he needs to take over the firm from his father one of these days, he must go to Amsterdam. Naturally this means the end of their affair, lovely though it seems to have been for both. Marriage is out of the question—not even Anna had hoped for that. He must marry well, and will be leaving in a few days. He kisses her twice, unwilling to go yet unable to resist the pressure that being a Buddenbrook imposes on him. "Look," he tells her, "one is borne along." He is beginning to feel, even as a young man, family bonds as chains.

Taken together, these kisses amount to very little. All other love scenes take place behind an impenetrable curtain of discretion. When Hugo Weinschenk, who is engaged to Tony's daughter, Erika, makes a little free with his fiancée's cheeks or arms at the Buddenbrook dinner table, the family assiduously overlooks his gaffes and makes some desperately bright remarks. They regard such uninhibited conduct as highly inappropriate, and Mann invites his readers to agree with him.

MANN'S RETICENCE IS NOT A SYMPTOM OF TIMIDITY BUT an element in his design. Passionate love has only a modest claim on the attention of the Buddenbrook family. Tony must forswear Morten, Thomas must leave Anna. Old Johann Buddenbrook had loved his wife: *"L'année la plus heureuse de ma vie,"* he had noted in the family album that little Hanno would disfigure many years later. But then she had died in childbirth, and his second marriage had been a rational, comfortable business transaction. His son's marital arrangements had been cast in the same mold. "His union, should he be honest about it," Mann interjects, "had not exactly been what one calls a love match. His father had tapped him on the shoulder and called his attention to the daughter of the rich Kröger, who brought the firm a handsome dowry. He had heartily agreed and had from then on respected his wife as the companion that God had entrusted to him." And both had lived together without visible strains.

The calculations of the fathers were handed down to the sons. The younger Johann Buddenbrook will impose the same businesslike proceeding on his beloved daughter, Tony, as though to justify belatedly his own prudent arrangements with love and marriage. Mann does not let the reader forget for an instant that Grünlich—a name meaning "greenish"—is a disagreeable young fellow, unctuous, assiduous, a consummate practitioner of the arts of dignified self-presentation and of sheer perseverance. He would have been a suitable partner for those canting, forever hungry Nonconformist preachers that Dickens pilloried in *Bleak House.* Once Johann Buddenbrook has made what he thinks are careful inquiries, once he has been made to believe that Herr Grünlich is a solid and promising young merchant, he virtually forces his daughter to sell herself to the man from Hamburg. And he enlists his wife in his anxious domestic campaign, a mixture of moral suasion, soft authoritarianism, self-deception, and frank avowals of his true reasons. "As you know," he tells her, "I can only urgently desire this marriage; it can only bring advantages to the family and to the firm." He has inspected Grünlich's balance sheets and is convinced that the young merchant has amassed a small fortune. Now that the Buddenbrook business has been slow for some time,

Tony's husband-to-be is most welcome. "Our daughter is marriageable and in a position to make a *partie*"—a French word for an international desire for a match that will bring a hefty dowry on the bride's, or a substantial bank balance on the groom's part. All else sinks into insignificance.

Johann Buddenbrook's infallible weapon of persuasion is his appeal to family pride, which Tony feels as keenly as does her father. She is, he tells her, a link in a long chain, and her membership in the clan imposes sacred obligations. Though utterly ignorant of life (as much as of sex), she is more perceptive than her parents in seeing through Grünlich; but they instruct her to distrust her feelings: she is young, inexperienced, they tell her, unfit to know her own inclinations—another instance just how little regard her family has for the deeper emotions. Her mother, no doubt recalling her own history, discounts Tony's aversion to her suitor: more positive sentiments for him will come with the passage of time, "I assure you." But her parents do not need to strain in order to co-opt her into the Buddenbrook ideology. It has been hers all along.

Tony's commitment to the family creed helps her to dismiss her promises to Morten with an exercise of the Buddenbrook will. Her pledge had been sincere, but once paternal authority urges a different decision upon her, it fades away. In Tony's mind, love for the Buddenbrook credo and love for her father merge. After the lavish wedding ceremony, already ensconced in the carriage that will take the couple off to their honeymoon, she impulsively, "ruthlessly," clambers over her husband to bid Johann Buddenbrook farewell once more. "She embraced her father passionately," Mann writes. "'Adieu, Papa, my good Papa!' And then she whispered very softly: 'Are you satisfied with me?'" He was. He had every reason to be.

The Buddenbrooks' determined search for a *partie,* then, is an

integral element in their way of life. As I have suggested, they con-
found family with firm, firm with family. And Tony will consistently live by this faith. When Grünlich shows himself to be as
dishonest as he was unlovable—one wonders just what kind of
books Johann Buddenbrook could have inspected—Tony's father
comes to take his daughter home, beset with feelings of guilt for
having forced upon her a husband she had justly found abhorrent.
But in dissolving her marriage, Tony is resolute against any financial rescue of Grünlich: none of her family's funds shall be used
to bail out her husband, faced though he is with irreparable disgrace. In late nineteenth-century Germany, a bankruptcy really
was a bankruptcy. She will divorce the man and move back to her
parents. Far from blaming her father, she finds that she is fonder
of him than ever. Earlier, Mann notes, Tony "had felt more timid
respect than tenderness" for her father. But now, free once more,
she is proud of him, touched by his solicitude, and, in turn, her
father "redoubled his love" for her. Nothing seemed more reas-
suring for Tony, who needed affection, than to regress to the first
object of her love.

THE SINGLE DEVIATION FROM THIS MERCANTILE
outlook, the marriage of Thomas Buddenbrook to Gerda
Arnoldsen, turns out to be not much of an exception at all. The
exuberant first encounter of the pair in Amsterdam, followed by
Thomas's energetic decision, "this one and no other," promises the
advent of romantic love. But passion is, at least for Thomas, com-
patible with making pointed inquiries. Writing to his mother that
he has at last found the woman he is determined to marry, he raises
the delicate subject of the *partie*. And he concedes that Gerda's

father is a millionaire. Which motive guided him, he asks himself, and cannot settle the question. He loves her "enthusiastically," but, he adds, "I certainly don't intend to descend into myself enough to discover whether, and how much, the large dowry, which they whispered into my ear in pretty cynical fashion when I was first introduced, contributed to my enthusiasm." He is sure that he loves Gerda Arnoldsen and that her father's money does not diminish his attachment to her. The reader has the uncomfortable feeling that his affection for Anna in the flower shop had been purer.

For, in marriage, the couple's love is cool, a little tense, built from the outset on an informal treaty of mutual forbearance that guarantees the lovely Gerda a domain of freedom and silence. It seems a little odd: her appearance, as Mann meticulously describes it, almost promised a more passionate union. She is tall, voluptuously built, red-haired (generally believed to be a sign of banked erotic fires), with shining teeth and a sensual mouth, altogether an "elegant, strange, captivating and mysterious beauty." Though unmistakably "northern" in her origins, she has something exotic in her looks, rather like the Anna that Thomas Buddenbrook had put aside. Gerda's splendid eyes, set close together, are hooded by fine bluish shadows, hinting at dark secrets and unknown threats. These bluish shadows are, in Mann's fashion, a feature that her doomed son will inherit from her. Of all the leitmotifs that crowd *Buddenbrooks,* at times to excess, that of Gerda's—and Hanno's—shadowed eyes is the most portentous. Somehow they seem to underscore the central theme of the novel, proclaimed in the subtitle—*Decay of a Family*—and amply carried through in the text.

Gossips in town had been puzzled by this marriage, but felt compelled to admit that it must have been a love match after all. Their perception was shallow. Mann notes that "of love, of that which one understands by love, there was from the beginning precious little between them as far as anyone could see. Rather, from the beginning, one had noticed nothing but courtesy in their relationship, a correct and respectful courtesy, quite extraordinary between husband and wife," not a symptom of alienation but of an odd "tacit, deep mutual intimacy." That was true at first, but in later years, the couple discarded the ultimate intimacy as they chose to occupy separate bedrooms. It is not the business of a critic to second-guess an author, but a Realist has an obligation not to violate the laws of probability; looking at what we know of this implausible pair, one may wonder just what she saw in him.

Gerda Buddenbrook is the most puzzling personage in *Buddenbrooks*. Mann kept her perplexing character intact by never entering her mind and keeping her distant from the others. He almost invariably reports her interventions in indirect speech. In contrast to her husband, to whose growing depression, increasing nervousness, and premature aging Mann devotes pages of disheartening detail, Gerda is a virtual cipher. She sits with her family, when she is present at all, embroidery in hand, watches them with those watchful eyes ringed by bluish shadows as they gossip, reminisce, or quarrel, and makes no comment. Almost the longest speech her creator gives her is a response to an ignorant remark of her husband's about music. "Thomas, once and for all," she begins her little diatribe, "of music as art you will never understand anything," and more, for a paragraph of gently spoken but devastating dismissal.

Gerda Buddenbrook loves music ardently and expertly. It is perhaps the passion that attaches her most strongly to her only child. She is close to her father, the other man in her life, for a very similar reason: she had enjoyed playing duets on the violin with him. And it was perhaps her bond with Mijnheer Arnoldsen that had kept her to the advanced age of twenty-seven from accepting offers of marriage until Thomas Buddenbrook found favor in her sight. Then, after some eighteen years of marriage, she begins to see a great deal of a young officer, Lieutenant von Throta, whose frequent visits to the house make her husband almost faint with jealousy. What entangles the two is a shared devotion to music; her husband's failure to value music as anything better than entertainment permanently excludes him from the innermost circle of her sensibility.

Thomas Buddenbrook's nemesis, as Mann depicts him, is something of a phenomenon. He plays the piano, the violin, the viola, the cello, and the flute, "all of them excellently." When the dreaded visitor arrived, carefully avoiding the master of the house, the helpless husband would sit in his office, listening, as "in the salon above him the harmonies surged amid singing, lamenting and superhuman jubilation, rose as it were with convulsively outstretched, folded hands and after all the mad and vague ecstasies sank down to weakness and sobs into night and silence." That was bad enough. But the worst the involuntary listener had to endure was silence, the "long, long silence" upstairs, interrupted by no sound, no steps. "Then Thomas Buddenbrook sat and was so frightened that he sometimes groaned softly." Are the two fanatics for music having an affair? Mann, who knows everything, will not say.

Music, we know, claimed a prominent place in nineteenth-century middle-class culture, and it was often a serious preoccupation, diligently practiced and lovingly pursued. Publishers trying to satisfy an insatiable demand threw onto the market vast quantities of sheet music, including highly popular piano transcriptions

for two or four hands of quartets, overtures, arias, even sym-
phonies. That is how industrious, often highly competent ama-
teurs gained access at home to compositions written for the
concert hall. The piano, the violin, the voice were, in untold numbers of bourgeois families, sources of pleasure and civilized sociability; their reputation as so many traps that marriageable maidens
set for eligible bachelors is largely unobserved. An unmarried
young man with a pleasing baritone or reasonably proficient in the
cello was welcome in middle-class households even if marriage
was the furthest thing from his (or their) mind. Mann himself was
a respectable violinist, and, as his novellas and essays attest,
attached to music the significance that religion would have for a
believer. Throughout *Buddenbrooks*, music works as the harbin-
ger and the agent of Eros, always electrifying, always risky, always
a discomfiting intrusion into, a kind of reproach to, mundane bourgeois activities. At the end, after Gerda Buddenbrook has been
widowed and lost her only child, she will return to Amsterdam to
play duets with her beloved father once again.

BUDDENBROOKS MAY BE THIN IN KISSES, BUT THE WAY
that Mann handles music in the novel is a reminder that it is at
heart a deeply erotic fiction. Yet this quality emerges in unexpected
places. The idea that music has its roots in human sexuality is as
old as Plato's *Symposium*. In his first novel, then, Mann stands in
a long tradition. The only orgasmic moments he admits to the book
come when Hanno is at the piano. He tastes in his diffident way
from the sexual sources of art. It is his eighth birthday. Though his
patience with practicing is limited and his progress on the piano
laborious, he likes to score effects by prolonging and intensifying

pleasures. He dreams, hovering over the keyboard, improvising little pieces. One of these, with a highly unorthodox coda, he refuses
to revise despite the protests of his benevolent, musically conservative piano teacher.

Playing his favorite composition for his family, he is pale with a
kind of intoxication. "And now came the finale, Hanno's beloved
finale, which crowned the whole with its primitive elevation. Soft
and pure as a bell, tremolo, sounds the e-minor chord, pianissimo,"
caressed, enveloped by his mother's violin accompaniment. "It
grew, it rose, it swelled slowly, slowly; Hanno introduced, forte,
the dissonant c-sharp, leading back to the original key, and while
the Stradivarius"—it has, of course, to be a Stradivarius—"heav-
ing and resonant, surges above this c-sharp too, he raises the dis-
sonance with all his might up to fortissimo."

But Hanno is not ready for the denouement, not quite yet. "He
denied himself the resolution, he kept it from himself and his listeners. What would it be, this resolution, this enchanting and liberated dissolution in b-major? Happiness beyond compare, a
satisfaction of rapturous sweetness. Peace! Bliss! The kingdom of
heaven! . . . Not yet . . . not yet! Just one more moment of delay,
of hesitation, of tension, which must become intolerable so that
the gratification may be all the more delicious. . . . Still a last, a
very last tasting of this pressing and driving yearning, this appetite
of the whole being, this most extreme and convulsive tension of
the will which yet denied itself satisfaction and deliverance,
because he knew: happiness is only a moment." Only then, bur-
dened with premature wisdom, does the eight-year-old permit
himself consummation. "Hanno's upper body slowly straightened
itself up, his eyes grew quite large, his closed lips trembled, with
a spasmodic tremor he drew in the air through his nostrils . . . and

then bliss could no longer be held back. It came, came over him, and he did not resist it any longer. His muscles relaxed, exhausted and overwhelmed his head sank onto his shoulders, his eyes closed, and a melancholy, almost anguished smile of inexpressible rapture played about his mouth." The Stradivarius, Mann reports, keeps the boy company right to the end, the son's duet with his mother continuing to the climax until the boy reaches the aftermath, happy and drained, entering realms of closeness to his mother that she had denied her husband.*

This erotic experience seems to be quite premature for an eight-year-old. But, unduly precocious or not, whether intended as a representation of a solitary gratification or one with a partner, it is designed as an account of a sexual consummation, skillfully delayed. That something like this was in Mann's mind emerges from a recapitulation he allows himself. All his writing life enamored of leitmotifs, we know, he reiterates this sexual motif, too, late in the novel. Seven years after Hanno's little birthday concert, having spent a long and strenuous day at school, he enjoys an "orgy"—the word is Mann's—as he improvises at the piano, this time without his mother. He is exploring a simple motif of his own devising, again, like his earlier composition, emotional, wild, untrammeled. Again he withholds the climax with an ambivalent longing for delay and reward. His playing, Mann comments, is a "submersion in appetite." The theme soars, with its "flood of cacophonies" rising, dropping, pressing forward, striving toward an "unutterable end which must come, must come now, this very moment, during

---

*The musicologist Walter Frisch has pointed out to me that Hanno's fantasia is an almost literal inversion of the "Tristan chord" that Wagner uses throughout *Tristan und Isolde*. If imitation is the highest form of flattery, even a manipulated imitation speaks of high admiration.

this frightful climax, since the languishing oppression has grown intolerable, the spasms of yearning could not be prolonged any more; it came, as though a curtain were being torn, doors springing open, thorn hedges opening of themselves, walls of flame collapsing into themselves." And afterwards a jubilant resolution and fulfillment. Then Hanno sounds the first motif again to let it celebrate an orgy of its own, in a mixture of brutality and sanctity, and, at the same time, something ascetic and religious, with a perverse insatiability, until he has sucked the last sweetness from the music, down to satiety, weariness, disgust. After that, he sits at the piano in silence, his chin on his chest and his hands in his lap. Later he will have supper, play a game of chess with his mother, go to his room to practice on his silent harmonium until after midnight. It has been a long and tiring day for Hanno Buddenbrook. The next morning he falls ill with typhoid.

Once again, in the midst of these sensual musical riots, we think of Antonia in Offenbach's *Tales of Hoffmann,* who permits an evil spirit to seduce her into a perverse, suicidal musical performance which she knows will kill her. But, typically, Mann reverses this tale: it is rather because Hanno is fated to die that he has afflicted him with a measure of musical talent. Hanno's love of music is a symptom of his alienation from the bourgeois world of his fathers, a signal of its inescapable decline.

DEATH-DEALING EROS INSINUATES HIMSELF INTO *Buddenbrooks* in yet another unorthodox way, glancingly, shyly, but unmistakably. It almost looks like a casual or inadvertent episode deserving no particular attention. But Thomas Mann, the most self-conscious of stylists, did not permit careless touches, or mere accidents, to enter his work. Hanno is on his deathbed; his end, like that of the novel, is near. He no longer recognizes anyone, until his favorite classmate, the impoverished Kai, Count von Mölln, virtually forces himself into the sickroom. Like Hanno, Kai was a boy who disliked school, and their bond was close, isolating them from their fellows. Hearing his friend's voice, Hanno smiles, knowing who is with him. And Kai incessantly kisses his dying friend's hands. When the Buddenbrook women in the closing chapter talk of Hanno and his final hours, they speak about this strange and touching scene, and, Mann reports, they think about it for a while.

Mann refuses to divulge just what they thought, but the brief interlude calls for comment. His own father, senator in Lübeck and eminent grain merchant, had died ten years before the publication of *Buddenbrooks,* when Thomas was sixteen, and his mother had moved to Munich, taking him and his younger siblings with her. In his will, the senator had decreed that the firm be dissolved; he had been realistic enough to see that neither his eldest son, Heinrich, nor "Tommy" would grow into effective men of commerce. When Thomas Mann in these years spoke of himself as ridden by a bad conscience, he tempted his interpreters to take these guilt feelings as evidence of a good son who had not been good enough, turning his back on a career in business to make himself into an artist.

There is something to this reading. With half his heart, Mann always remained a patrician of Lübeck. But his feelings of guilt ran deeper than having let his father down. He was haunted by anxieties about his homoerotic appetites. In the letter to Heinrich

Mann of March 1901, in which he had defined *Buddenbrooks* as a mixture of music, metaphysics, and adolescent eroticism, he also noted that his depression had been lifted by a new "happiness of the heart." That happiness originated in an infatuation with the painter Paul Ehrenberg. But he reassured his brother: "It is not a love story, at least not in the common meaning, but about a friendship—O astonishment!—a friendship understood, reciprocated, worthwhile."

Ehrenberg was not Mann's earliest amorous enthusiasm. Reminiscing in 1931, he assigned to his fellow pupil Armin Martens the honor of being his "first love." That was in 1889; Mann was then thirteen. "A more tender, more blissful-painful one has never again fallen to my lot," he confessed to a friend of his schooldays in 1955, the last year of his life. "It may sound ridiculous, but I have preserved the memory of this innocent passion like a treasure." He left a sly memento to Martens in *Buddenbrooks* by giving the first name "Morten" to the medical student in Tony's young life.

During his adolescence, about the year that Thomas Mann discovered these proclivities, homosexual love was, in the words of Oscar Wilde's paramour, Lord Alfred Douglas, the love that dared not speak its name. Nor did it become respectable during his lifetime, not even for avant-garde artists, to whom more was permitted than to ordinary bourgeois. André Gide, who wrote freely about his "orientation," was a spectacular exception. Around 1900, brooding to his closest friends about his cravings, Mann commended, and seems to have practiced, asceticism. He professed to find sexuality, all sexuality, hateful; a serious literary man, he said, must turn away from it.

Yet his passion for men, suppressed though never quite repressed, toyed with him; his feminine identifications (to use psychoanalytic jargon for a moment) invaded his masculine ones and would take control. He had lengthy bouts with homoerotic yearnings in the years of World War I and intermittently after—there was a time when he found his growing son Klaus handsome enough, he confessed to his diary, to be in love with him. As late as 1950, at a resort hotel in Zurich—he was seventy-five—he became infatuated with a good-looking waiter: Mann's hopes to see him again soon, his brief exchanges with "Franzl," dominated his diaries for some months.

He was not incapable of loving women. He responded to feminine beauty, especially when decorated with brains. His wooing of the attractive and intelligent Katja Pringsheim, who became his wife in 1905, was long and determined. He fathered six children with her. To be sure, his diaries reveal that the temperature of his love for her was often cool. And the well-known fact that her father was a millionaire did not tarnish his feelings for Katja. Much like Thomas Buddenbrook, Mann loved the woman he chose to marry as best he could, and his diaries document that, in addition to her forbearance with his failures in bed and his complicated erotic history, time and again his bond with her was, he judged, very sensual.

Whatever his sexual needs, he learned how to sublimate them. After experimenting with short fiction and poems, he first came to public notice with a long story, *Der kleine Herr Friedemann*, published in 1897. This "breakthrough," as he called it later, gave him confidence in his mastery as a writer to manipulate words, characters, and plots, both to communicate and to conceal. "For some time," he wrote to his adoring friend Otto Grautoff in the same year, "it seems to me as though I have got elbow room, as though I have found ways and means of expressing myself freely, of living to the full, and though I used to need a diary to relieve myself in complete privacy, I now find fictional forms and masks suitable for the public to let out my love, my hatred, my pity, my contempt, my pride, my scorn and my accusations"—he could have added, "my sexual desires." For he liberally employed his masks to vent, and at the same time to disguise, his homoerotic appetites.

At times, he discovered them where no one else suspected their presence. In 1919, a year after he published *Reflections of an Unpolitical Man,* he noted in his diary that he had no doubt that the book, that exercise in cultural politics, was "also an expression of my sexual inversion." Readers of Mann's fiction well know that he populated the most famous among his writings with adolescent homoerotic infatuations, none of them consummated: the eponymous Tonio Kröger for Hans Hansen, and Hans Castorp for Pribislav Hippe in *The Magic Mountain.* And Gustav von Aschenbach, the protagonist for Mann's best-known novella, *Death in Venice,* is an aging writer whose love for a beautiful Polish boy, Tadzio, will condemn him to death. The moments when Kai kisses the hands of his dying friend, Hanno, are an early, delicate expression of what gave Mann his bad conscience.

THIS RAPID SURVEY OF MANN'S SEXUAL AMBIVALENCE should help to define his animus against his privileged family history, a complicated amalgam of psychological, literary, and social needs and grievances. In *Buddenbrooks,* these complexities find expression in the conflicts between two representative figures, the brothers Thomas and Christian Buddenbrook. The two have sometimes been taken to stand for both sides of Thomas Mann's personality, or for the battling brothers Thomas and Heinrich Mann.

But that is too direct, too simple a translation of Thomas Mann's torn nature. The brothers serve, and clash over, larger issues. Christian, we know, is spectacularly unsuccessful, an irritating neurotic and a self-serving wastrel. He consorts with rakes from his own class, spoiled patricians' sons, and keeps an unsuitable mistress. Thomas, we also know, could not be more different, being painfully self-disciplined and public-spirited. Each is unhappy in his own way. In their contrasting fashion, the brothers live out two incompatible styles of living: the *Bürger* against the bohemian.

The furious quarrel that erupts between them after earlier skirmishes, with a kind of tasteless inevitability right after their mother's death, forces their long-standing rivalry to the surface. With her body lying in state next door, the fraternal confrontation starts, symbolic for a mercantile family, not over her love but over her "things." Christian suspects that his brother is arrogating to himself too much of her precious silverware, and from this objection the conflict escalates. It is not really about a few spoons or a silver teapot: the battle between the gospels of self-denying work and self-indulgent pleasure is joined. Thomas, who has occasional insights into himself, concedes that he has at times felt the temptation to abandon the strenuous life for a more relaxed existence. His stiff upper lip—Mann has made this point repeatedly and at length—has proved to be disappointing and exhausting. "I have become as I am," he tells Christian in the midst of their rancorous duel, "because I did not want to become like you. If I have inwardly shunned you, that was because I had to guard myself against you, because your being and your existence are a danger to me. . . . I am telling the truth." During all this contention, Gerda Buddenbrook sits by attentively and silently. Was her husband thinking of Anna, the girl in the flower shop?

As the Olympian observer, Mann renders this fraternal warfare with admirable evenhandedness. Both men are deeply flawed, Christian, who will end up in a mental institution, more obviously than Thomas. But the fate of Thomas is in its way hardly less pathetic. We recall how in the last years of his life, he had grown increasingly embittered, compelled to conceal his misery behind the facade of the thriving merchant and the happy husband, even though the truth is sadly different as he contemplates his cool wife, his disappointing son, his troubled business, his meaningless public obligations. "It was empty within him, and he saw no stimulating plan and no absorbing undertaking to which he might devote himself with joy and satisfaction." That a more modern, less scrupulous capitalist should be overtaking him is only the final insult. He has gained weight, suffers from sleeplessness, fatigue, and an incurable restlessness. With Lieutenant von Throta constantly in the house—it seems to be no secret to anyone—he has come to seem a little ridiculous to local busybodies who decide that he is over the hill.

But one day not long before his death he finds a chance for deliverance from burdens he can hardly bear. Mann was proud of this passage, and would offer it as proof that *Buddenbrooks* was better than some mindless family chronicle. Thomas Buddenbrook comes upon a book, the second volume of a famous work of philosophy he had once bought as a bargain. He takes it into the garden and begins to read, having no idea that he is holding part of Schopenhauer's *The World as Will and Idea*—the title page is missing. He is utterly fascinated. Unused to reading philosophy, he fails to grasp much of the argument until he comes upon a long chapter on death, and reads it word for word, with a concentration he has not mustered for years.

Numb with excitement, he goes to bed weeping, liberated somehow from his world. Individuality, petty worries, jealousies, what do they matter? "Have I hoped to live on in my son? In a personality still weaker, more timid, more vacillating? Childish, deluded folly! Why do I need a son? . . . Where shall I be when I am dead? But it is so radiantly clear, so overwhelmingly simple! I shall be in all those who have ever said 'I,' say it, and will say it: *but especially in those who say it more fully, more forcefully, more cheerfully. . . .*" Amid tears he says into his pillow: "I shall live!" But as he wakes up next morning, he finds his old life reclaiming him. He plans to go back to the book that had offered him an entirely new way of living and dying; but he will never look at it again. That unknown philosopher demands too much from him. "His bourgeois instincts," writes Mann, "rose up against it, as did his vanity: the fear of playing an odd and ridiculous role." Thomas has wasted his last opportunity to escape his fate.*

IN THE YEARS OF *BUDDENBROOKS,* THOMAS MANN TOYED with the fashionable antithesis of avant-garde art versus conventional life. He saw art—novels, poems, paintings, music, and the

---

*After the end of World War I, Thomas Mann's view of life altered dramatically. In 1922, in a controversial lecture, "Of the German Republic," he declared that his infatuation with death was over. And in 1925, in *The Magic Mountain,* he has its hero, Hans Castorp, declare in a famous sentence: "For the sake of goodness and love, man shall not concede to death mastery over his thoughts." That is important for any full appraisal of Mann's mind, but for a study of the profit that a historian may glean from *Buddenbrooks,* it is of course irrelevant.

rest of high culture—as the mortal enemy of the bourgeois, a label he thought synonymous with "philistine." Setting up the kind of conflict he then found irresistible, he argued that the middle classes, responding to this challenge, distrusted all art that was in any way demanding and did their utmost to co-opt or to destroy it. Art, on this reading, is the brother of love, both alike irrational and subversive forces that disrupt the comfortable arrangements pleasing to the self-satisfied, incurably vulgar bourgeoisie.

But even as early as 1901, Mann could not sustain unqualified confrontations of art with materialism, passion with reason, alienated bohemianism with patrician sturdiness. His ambivalence was too keen for that. On the one hand, he could not wholly separate himself from his heritage. "I am a townsman, a *Bürger,* a child and great-grandchild of German middle-class culture," he wrote. He was proud of his forebears who had been artisans in Nürnberg and "merchants of the Holy Roman Empire." Yet he came to see that the absolute contrast between the *Bürger*—unbending, old-fashioned, essentially German—and the bourgeois—mobile, iconoclastic, essentially French—could not be sustained. We know that he liked to think of his creation, Thomas Buddenbrook, as a kind of modern hero, a man who had made the transition, strange as this might sound, from driven *Bürger* to driven bourgeois, with the lure of art another beckoning complication. Still, Mann was certain that he could not and would not be a merchant like his father and grandfather before him.

We can measure the depth of Mann's mixed feelings with one of his most successful long stories, *Tonio Kröger,* to which he turned after completing *Buddenbrooks:* the novel and the novella belong to the same mental universe. And the novella remained his favorite: in 1931, after publishing a substantial body of work including *The Magic Mountain,* he called *Buddenbrooks* "my most popular book." It "will remain so," he believed, but, he added, "at the bottom of my heart I am more attached to *Tonio Kröger.*" It is easy to see why: the novella is the most openly autobiographical fiction he ever wrote, rehearsing with impressive subtlety the relation of high culture to middle-class life. Tonio is a patrician's son from the north, who in his passion for literature goes south to Italy and then to Munich—just as Thomas Mann had done.

He has returned to Germany, and continues to feel himself to be an outsider. In a frank, wide-ranging conversation with his good friend, the painter Lisaweta Iwanowna, he confesses to her his love of life and his uncomfortable sense that his chosen vocation, literature, is not a profession but a curse. It brings loneliness, insecurity, distance from the pleasures and the security of ordinary people. Her honest reply to his plaint: You are a *Bürger, a Bürger* who has gone astray, lost his way. A little hurt, he acknowledges the justice of her charge. Half a year later he still thinks of it, and writes to her: "I stand between two worlds, am at home in neither." Hence his life, he tells her, is a little hard. But precisely because he is a *Bürger,* however lost, precisely because he loves "the human, the living, the common," he can do his work as a serious writer. And Tonio—that is to say, Mann—drops a hint, no more, that it should be possible to find a way of making peace between the two warring camps.

But that accord would come for him only, to the extent that it did, many years after—too late for the reader who knows only *Buddenbrooks* and *Tonio Kröger.* And the intimation of that later synthesis was overwhelmed by the pressure of World War I. Driven by patriotic fervor and the sense that the Germanic virtues of

Items that you checked out

Title: Clair de lune [sound recording] :
    Debussy favourites.
ID: 31010001173220
Due: February-08-17

Title:
 Hamlet [videorecording] / directed by
 Tony Richardson.
ID: 31010001134065
Due: February-08-17

Title:
 Savage reprisals : Bleak house, Madame
 Bovary, Buddenbrooks / Peter Gay.
ID: 17047903
Due: February-08-17

Items checked out this session: 3
January-18-17
Checked out: 4
Overdue: 0
Hold requests: 0
Ready for pickup: 0

Renew 604-925-7404 or
http://wvml.ca/renew
Mon-Thu 10-9 Fri 10-6 Sat 10-5 Sun 10-5
(Closed Sundays July-August)

inwardness and moral depth were under attack from calculating, mercantile societies, he regressed to absolute, primitive opposites: friend against enemy, the Central Powers against the Allies, the artist against the philistine. He composed a vast polemic, *Betrachtungen eines Unpolitischen—Reflections of an Unpolitical Man,* published in 1918, part of his quarrel with his liberal, cosmopolitan brother Heinrich. It was not until the early 1920s that he committed himself to the Weimar Republic, that endangered experiment in democracy hated by many and loved, if at all, with only a moderate affection.

Mann's extreme thinking in antitheses, which governed his political and cultural choices in the time of *Buddenbrooks,* recalls Flaubert's indiscriminate hatred of what he liked to call the bourgeoisie. At times, the author of *Madame Bovary* knew better: he could even muster a certain affection for his creatures Bouvard and Pécuchet; they were idiots, but, he insisted, they were *his* idiots. And he could quite arbitrarily exempt friends like the publisher Charpentier and his family from the stigma of being bourgeois. Still, these were rare moments of insight. This is where Mann differed from Flaubert: Mann got over it.

FOR THE HISTORIAN, THIS CANNOT BE THE FINAL word. However comprehensive Mann's claim that his representation of the Buddenbrooks had anticipated scholarly sociologists like Max Weber and others and offered a collective portrait of the modern *Bürgertum,* his first novel remains, more than one might think at first glance, a highly personal testimonial. There were, in those days, middle-class German families less obviously doomed than the Buddenbrooks, less fated to succeed than the Hagenströms. What is more, and what is central, is that Thomas Mann did not write this family saga from a neutral corner.

In short, acting on his own, without needing guidance from Dickens and Flaubert, Mann produced this novel as an act of retribution. Both his predecessors had confronted their society and found it wanting; both had made great novels from their political hatreds. So did Mann. He said so explicitly: "The pitiless precision of the description," he wrote about *Buddenbrooks* in 1906, "is the artist's sublime *revenge* on his experience"—a revenge on a father disappointed in his son's failure to succeed him, and a revenge on a reputable, upright society that expected him to be more infallibly masculine than he turned out to be.

Some of Mann's most significant final gestures feature this revenge motif with astonishing clarity. Not long before his death, he destroyed several of his thoroughgoing and forthcoming diaries. The surviving ones have served recent biographers to exploit, in lip-licking detail, the private secret of which students of Mann had only a few hints to go on: his homosexual urges. But their revelations only deepen another secret: why did he not destroy all of these daily confessions? He only provided that they not be opened until twenty years after his death. What did he want the world to know, and why? I read the surviving diaries as a posthumous revenge on his audience and on his family alike, the last act—one senses his ironic smile—of a mutinous patrician.

EPILOGUE

Truths of Fictions

SOME TIME IN 1913, NOT LONG AFTER *DU CÔTÉ DE CHEZ Swann* was published, Marcel Proust, hot with the hubris of the writer whose creative energies were flowing freely, told an interviewer that writing their fictions, novelists create new worlds. To which Rebecca West tartly objected: "one of the damn things is enough." There is something admirable about Proust grandly promoting writers into a kind of divinity; major modern poets like Wallace Stevens have echoed this presumption. But West had a sound argument on her side. The world the Realist novelist creates is the same as the historian's world, only reached by his own paths. What Elizabeth Bishop well said about poets also applies to novelists: they too place imaginary toads into real gardens. And even the toads look suspiciously like the real thing.

This Realist outlook implies a position about truth in fiction and fiction in history that I want to make explicit in some concluding observations. These are deep waters, I know, and I can only skim the surface here. In retrospect, it seems to have been an intelligent move on the part of "jesting Pilate," as Francis Bacon tells us, to evade the issue. "What is truth?" he asked, "and would not stay for an answer." Among most contemporary literary critics and the historians troubled by the problem of knowledge, the very definition of global terms like "fact" or "truth" remains highly contentious.

But not among philosophers in our time. With the exception of the small band of pragmatists, virtually all others subscribe to a critical Realism, which holds that, for all the obstructions to accurate observation, all the inducements to self-deception, there is a real world out there, independent of anyone's mind. One of the damn things is enough. If truths are elusive, facts hard to pin down, it does not follow that they do not exist. The much-instanced tree that falls in a forest unobserved makes the same crashing noise it makes if there is someone standing near it. Speaking for this overwhelming consensus, Sir Karl Popper put the case a little brutally when he assailed philosophical Idealism for its arrogant belief that "it is my mind which creates this beautiful world," which seemed to him a form of megalomania. Scores of philosophers have said the same thing, though rather more politely.

Even Thomas Kuhn, probably the twentieth century's most influential historian and philosopher of science, whose brave talk of paradigm shifts has been misappropriated by relativists, maintained that the external world is real, neither constructed nor invented. The English philosopher G. E. Moore, asked to justify his belief in the existence of an external world, simply held out his hands. There are more sophisticated ways of making the same assertion, but among scholars who professionally deal with such matters, the truth of truth—and of facts—is largely beyond dispute.

It is from this Realist position that I want to confront two critiques of historians' claims to truthfulness, one very old and very respectable, the other very new and very subversive. They have nothing in common except their severity with the devotees of Clio. The first holds that novelists and poets reach higher—which is to say deeper—truths, truths that historians, pedestrian, document-ridden fact grubbers that they are, can never even approach. Had Aristotle not already maintained in his *Poetics* that poetry is more philosophical and of greater importance than history? Milan Kundera has offered a modern version of this position: "I'll never tire of repeating: The novel's sole *raison d'être* is to say what only the novel can say." This *"radical autonomy"* of fiction "allowed Franz Kafka to say things about our human condition (as it reveals itself in our century) that no social or political thought could ever tell us." Poor historians, limping along behind the profound insights accessible only to novelists!

All professional resentment apart, in elevating fiction over history, Aristotle—and Kundera—offer an attractive proposition. To readers of novels it feels right somehow; the novelist discovering for his or her readers the ways of humans in the world, their experience with others and themselves, can provide a profound shock of recognition: This is how people are! This is how they love and hate! This is how they decide or equivocate! A survey of the literary canon offers an impressive array of novelists, their antennas aquiver with fine discernment, who, putting their characters through their paces, have attained dazzling insights into human nature at work. Dostoyevsky plumbing the depths of guilt and redemption, Proust exploring variations on the calamities of jealous love, Henry James dissecting the subtlest nuances of thought, are only three instances of superlative discoverers of truths. Others come readily to mind. I am reminded of Freud's disclaimer that he had discovered the unconscious: as an avid reader he knew that imaginative writers—*Dichter*—had done so before him, leaving him with the task of turning intuitions into science. There is no denying that men and women of the imagination can glimpse hitherto unseen vistas through their creative imagination alone; though, I would insist, a modicum of knowledge helps a great deal.

I would insist also that when we laud the novelist's insights, we are speaking of his psychological acumen. In that vast area, the study of individual minds and collective mentalities, the novelist and the historian meet. For, whatever historians may say, they too, however amateurishly, are psychologists. In *Tom Watson: Agrarian Rebel* (1938), C. Vann Woodward, writing the life of a powerful Georgia populist, had to make credible a politician who had started out as a courageous, eloquent champion of the poor and reinvented himself as an incendiary racist appealing to the emotions of the mob. "I had no pat psychological theory," Woodward recalled, looking back, "no comprehensive explanation of the enigma that I could spell out with conviction." What he did have was a sensitive intelligence and a willingness to let the materials he unearthed work on him. And the book is a striking companion, with its insights into the minds of leader and led, to Robert Penn Warren's *All the King's Men* (1946), based on the career of Huey Long, a book that brilliantly illuminated the man who ruled Louisiana in the late 1920s and early 1930s ("I am the constitution!"). With two such gifted writers, one a historian and the other a novelist, every effort at comparative rankings is beside the point. They reached the same truths by different means.

THE SECOND CRITIQUE RAISES MORE UNEASINESS these days and deserves more thoroughgoing comment. The postmodernist invasion of the historian's natural habitat is quite impar-

tial: it denies the claims of both historians and novelists to veracity on the simple ground that there is no such thing as truth to
begin with. Everything, a work of history as much as a novel, is
only a text with its subtexts. Jacques Derrida, the guru of the postmodernists, and fashionable followers, like Gayatri Chakravorty
Spivak, have consistently maintained that texts have no stable
identity. Hence all texts, including historical texts, however solid
they may appear, are susceptible to the most variant readings.
Historians' Realism is an illusion.

It must seem strange to most historians that the postmodernists
among them find this a cause for celebration rather than lament.
The delightful stories a historian can tell, in Simon Schama's
words, "dissolve the certainty of events into the multiple possibilities of alternative narrations." Such cheerfulness runs counter to
the conventional wisdom among historians: they are trained, after
all, to do their utmost to eliminate as many alternative narrations
as possible to settle on the one that to their mind approaches the
truth most closely. Sir Lewis Namier, that combative specialist in
eighteenth-century English politics, said years ago that the historian's principal task is to discover how things did *not* happen. True
enough: students of the past probably expend more energy reject-
ing interpretations than offering them.

Hayden White, the most influential among postmodern historians, has driven the relativist perspective to its limits. "Historical
events," he writes, "are supposed to consist of or manifest a con-
geries of 'real' or 'lived' stories, which have only to be understood
or extracted from the evidence and displayed before the reader to
have their truth recognized immediately and intuitively." But this
is an illusion, an attitude "mistaken or at best misconceived.
Stories, like factual statements, are linguistic entities and belong

to the order of discourse." To postmodernists, facts are not discovered but created; their intellectual ancestors, going back at
least as far as Goethe, have long insisted that every fact is already
an interpretation. As a social construction, it is inherently shaped
by the dominant social myths that hold the historian (like the novelist) in their iron grip. Bias, blinkers, tunnel vision, blind spots,
all sorts of impediments to objectivity, are essential, in the very
nature of all human efforts to know; the student of the past is the
prisoner of his own personal history. On this view, writing history
is just another way of writing fiction.

AGAINST THIS SKEPTICISM I WANT TO UNDERSCORE THAT
the claim that there are no innocent facts, that they are all con-
taminated by the poison of partisanship, is wholly untenable. It is
refuted every day by the infinite number of facts and interpretations on which historians of all stripes are in accord. Apart from
its inherent absurdity, the postmodernist attempt to reduce to irrel-
evance the historian's pursuit of truth has practical consequences.
It would force the writers of facts and the writers of fiction into
an unwanted gunshot marriage. The modish advocacy of virtually
unchecked subjectivity would lead to a regression from the
autonomous status that historians had begun to assert in the eigh-
teenth century, to a retreat from territory energetically secured and
productively cultivated.* After a millennium of being in thrall to

*For some decades, starting in the 1930s, American historians were being bom-
barded with, though hardly persuaded by, prominent historians preaching the

theology, during which historians attributed the causes of events to the divine will at work, the eighteenth-century philosophes argued that the agency of nature and human activity alone can make a difference in the world.

This secularization of causes produced dividends for the historical profession. By late in the nineteenth century, they had come to see themselves, with real conviction if somewhat excessive confidence, as scientists. They granted that strongly held presuppositions—intellectual, political, theological—often infect free investigative curiosity. When, at the end of the nineteenth century, Lord Acton expressed the hope of finding a French, a German, and a British historian agreeing on an account of the battle of Waterloo, this seemed to his contemporaries a worthy but Utopian wish.

Which is to say that historians have needed no postmodernists to tell them that the standpoint of individual practitioners, in part unconscious, might impede an objective treatment of the past. They would say so as they happily exposed the partiality of others. But they would treat such traps on the way to truth as handicaps to be overcome rather than laws of human nature to be humbly obeyed. They must remain skeptical of Schama's "rather banal axiom" that "claims for historical knowledge must always be fatally circumscribed by the character and prejudices of its narrator." Rather banal it is, but "always" and "fatally"?

---

subjectivity of their craft. In 1931, Carl Becker shook up the profession with his witty presidential address, "Everyman His Own Historian," followed two years later by Charles A. Beard's "Written History as an Act of Faith." It is not difficult to refute the skepticism that Becker and Beard trumpeted but never practiced in their own work. But it leads to the thought that fortunately historians writing history normally disregard the dubious philosophical propositions they espouse when writing *about* history.

It is often possible to trace the underlying motives for a historian's choice of subject. The urge to defy one's elders or the urge to obey them, the enthusiastic undertaking of a difficult assignment or its anxious rejection, are only some of the reasons that may propel a scholar's researches in one direction or another. There are times of upheaval and calamities—the twentieth century was only too rich in them—when a historian cannot shake off early experiences; we have all met refugees from totalitarianism, at once horrified and fascinated by their travail, who have spent their career desperate to understand, to explain, perhaps compulsively to reenact, the traumas of their youth.

Yet there is a fundamental difference between the motives for tackling a subject and the results, between what scientists call the context of discovery and the context of justification. True, the reader can hardly expect a sympathetic biography of Martin Luther from a devout Roman Catholic or an appreciative life of Oliver Cromwell from a monarchist. Yet, rigorously schooled in the historian's vocation, this Catholic and this monarchist are prompted to set aside their starting points, to leave as it were their autobiography behind. Their professional superego is trained to anticipate what critics would be bound to unearth: the love or hatred that has dictated one historian's pen, the hidden agendas that have imposed unbalanced conclusions on another. The specter of potential reviewers sharpening their pencils, of peers mercilessly judging peers, has a remarkably sobering effect.

Nor is it critics alone who stay the hand of the impassioned partisan. Long decades ago, historians evolved an array of defensive techniques, which, though they do not guarantee pure objectivity, reduce the opportunity for bias whether blatant or understated.

The footnote and the bibliography are claims to sources really used and to passages quoted correctly and in context, both of them open to public scrutiny and diligent reexamination. They enroll the historian in a professional guild with well-established standards, standards themselves subject to scrutiny.

◩ NO PROCEDURE IS INFALLIBLE. FOR ALL THEIR VAST areas of consensus, historians notoriously disagree. But that is not a matter of fashion or unprofessional present-mindedness alone: one historian may mobilize documentation superior to what his competitors have used; another may approach a familiar subject with an unconventional auxiliary discipline (such as psychoanalysis) to arrive at an interpretation more comprehensive and more penetrating than those proposed by earlier researchers. Nor do strong ethical convictions necessarily frustrate the historian's attempt at fairness; a historian may believe that eating people is wrong and still try to do justice to cannibals. The American historian Thomas L. Haskell has put it trenchantly: "Objectivity is not neutrality." In fact, in the right hands, a certain way of looking at the world will only enlarge and sharpen, rather than limit, the historian's view of the past.

In short, historians' debates (without which the profession would be reduced to a boring recital of universally accepted facts) are all part of an unending collective enterprise trying to approx-, imate Lord Acton's exacting ideal: a thoroughly well-informed accord on the past. None of the objections raised to that ideal holds valid. To put it bluntly: there may be history in fiction, but there should be no fiction in history.

WHAT KIND OF HISTORY, THEN, DO NOVELISTS DO BEST? Their most promising way to truth lies in their ability to move between what I have called the large and the small, society and the individual. Consider once again Thomas Buddenbrook, the character whom Thomas Mann a little defiantly called a hero. He is both a distinctive, suffering person and a social type, an uneasy burgher who hesitantly embraces the fate of a modern bourgeois. His life, as Mann describes it, is uniquely his own, with his unhappy marriage, his remote, alien son, his boredom with public duties, his discovery of Schopenhauer, even his toothaches. But at the same time he represents many middle-class lives and not just in Lübeck. In other words, the novelist's most distinctive, most highly individualized personages may simultaneously represent more inclusive realities. It is not the events alone that the novelist can illuminate—for this, as I said at the beginning, the reader needs to consult second opinions—but their reception.

This is the way, through individual responses, that the novelist can visualize and effectively embody crowded events more spectacularly than an unadorned recital ever could. He—or she—must see them through the eyes of a single participant. Fabrice erring about the battlefield of Waterloo in Stendhal's *La Chartreuse de Parme* unfolds a confusing, almost incomprehensible scene of battle, typical of most battles; but it is through Fabrice's consciousness that Stendhal transmits this common reality with convincing immediacy. Flaubert's account in *L'Education sentimentale* of political enthusiasm unleashed in the

Paris of early 1848 reads like an essay on crowd psychology, but it manifests itself through highly individualized participants, through Frédéric Moreau and his friends.

Novels, to reiterate this essential if obvious point, are fictions, not monographs: Thackeray's Becky Sharp's career among men avid for sexual conquests in *Vanity Fair* provides access to English class politics in Napoleonic times, but she remains boldly, unforgettably herself. Effi Briest, the eponymous heroine of Theodor Fontane's best-known novel, lays bare the disproportionately high wages of sin in respectable imperial German society; but, a lovable victim, she lives and dies in the reader's mind as a touching, innocent young mother doomed by a single erotic misstep. If the protagonists of novels are simply individuals, the fiction they dominate will have nothing for the historian; if such protagonists are simply types, the novel in which they appear will not be a serious contribution to literature.

THE MOST IMPRESSIVE HISTORICAL WORK THAT modern novelists have done has been in the "dictator-novel." The genre is sizable and rapidly growing, most notably—for all too obvious reasons—among Latin American writers. Perhaps the most extraordinary example of this type is Gabriel García Márquez's *The Autumn of the Patriarch,* published in 1975. Since it raises the question of truth in fiction in its most dramatic form, it may serve to conclude this discussion. García Márquez, whose native Colombia had seen its share of political repression, had written about the impact of dictatorships almost from the beginning of his career, exhibiting the prudent silences, Aesopian circumlocutions, and sheer terror characteristic of them. But in *The Autumn of the Patriarch*, he deployed unconventional stylistic devices with exceptional finesse, and cast a far wider net.

In educating himself about despotism, García Márquez canvassed ancient history, elevating his theme to the historical phenomenon as such. "I learned a lot from Plutarch and Suetonius," he said in an interview in 1977, "as I did in general from all the biographers of Julius Caesar"; it helped him to design "that crazy quilt which is the old Patriarch, stitched together as he was from all the dictators in the history of man." He is far from principled purists who categorically separate fiction from fact, allowing no bridge between the two, and refusing to see the presence of the real world in fiction in defiance of the most palpable evidence. For his part, García Márquez freely acknowledges the force of real events in his novel, of truth on fiction. In his work (as in that of others), history is always in the back of his mind.

Yet the heart of *Autumn of the Patriarch* lies not with Julius Caesar but in South and Central America. The novel is not the portrait of a single despot, but, as García Márquez's sweeping formulation has it, "a synthesis of all the Latin American dictators, but especially those from the Caribbean." In short, it ranges beyond the sanguinary recent decades to what the novelist called "the phantoms of Latin America." After South and Central American countries had gained independence from Spain early in the nineteenth century, most of them veered between anarchy and authoritarianism, and some were run by bloodthirsty, superstitious megalomaniacs strutting in their fanciful uniforms. In his address accepting the Nobel Prize for Literature in 1982, García Márquez related some hair-raising anecdotes about their misrule that might have been funny if the whole history of Latin America were not so heavily steeped in blood.* His grim comment: "We have never had a moment of serenity." No doubt, García Márquez had overwhelmingly rich materials to draw on.

His novel recounts the life and death of an unnamed "Patriarch" in an unnamed country, probably Caribbean, addressed as "General." He exhibits all the traits expected in a despot—narcissism, brutality, sexual libertinism, a certain native shrewdness—and more: he is credited with performing miracles like changing the time of day and the weather at his command. Such supernatural acts are, of course, the hyperbole ingrained in Magical Realism, but they uncomfortably approach the sober, horrifying realities of real dictatorships. *The Autumn of the Patriarch* recalls the nineteenth-century Dominican politicians shopping around to find a buyer for their country: it has the General sell the sea that borders on his dominions. What Hilary Mantel said of the French Revolution holds for this despot and his half-imagined country even more strongly: anything that seems particularly unlikely is probably true.

What is historical, what invented in *The Autumn of the Patriarch*? The novel offers no easy answers and deliberately

---

*"General Antonio Lôpez de Santana, thrice dictator of Mexico, had the right hand he lost in the so-called War of the Cakes buried with all funereal pomp. General García Moreno governed Ecuador for sixteen years as an absolute monarch and his dead body, dressed in full-dress uniform and his cuirass with its medals, sat in state upon the presidential throne. General Maximilian Hernández Martinez, the theosophical despot of El Salvador who had thirty thousand peasants exterminated in a savage orgy of killing, invented a pendulum to discover whether food was poisoned and had the street lamps covered with red paper to combat an epidemic of scarlet fever. The monument to General Francisco Morazán, raised up in the main square of Tegucigalpa is, in reality, a statue of Marshall Ney which was bought in a repository of second-hand statues in Paris." "Solitude of Latin America," *New Readings*, 208.

undercuts the clues that it deigns to offer. Each of its six sections—
each a single flowing river of a paragraph—begins with the finding of the General's body and then veers back to his bizarre life.
There is no detectable dramatic time for the action: García
Márquez offers no dates, and introduces, along with American
marines, anachronistic figures like Christopher Columbus. Nor
does he assign the Patriarch any specific age; he is anywhere
between 107 and 232 years old. Most perplexing of all, the narrative voices García Márquez utilizes are bewildering in their flu-
idity. The speakers are anonymous and omniscient. For the most
part, they seem to be a member of the general public or perhaps
one of the officers close to the General. But others take up the
burden of the tale, among them the dictator's guards, a prostitute,
the Patriarch's mother, the Patriarch himself—or are these last,
crucial passages in the book not just speeches related by the collective voice? At times, simply to complicate these complications,
the novel shifts the identity of the narrator in midsentence.

   Until the last two or three pages, when there is a subtle shift in
tone though not in style, all the narrators speak in a matter-of-fact
tone, even in the horrendous episodes they report, a tone only
relieved, perhaps intensified, by García Márquez's macabre humor.
And he does not analyze the Patriarch's rule; he simply describes
it, one grotesque incident after another. On his last day on earth,
the President, addressed by Death, realizes that "after so many
years of sterile illusions he had begun to glimpse," but too late, "that
even the broadest and most useful of lives only reach the point of
learning how to live, he had learned of his incapacity to love. . . ."
As the book closes, "frantic crowds" hail "the jubilant news of his
death" and "the bells of glory that announced to the world the good
news that the uncountable time of eternity had come to an end."

It would be missing García Márquez's intentions to charge him with preaching the trite wisdom that, to survive tyranny, all one needs is love. He wants to drench the reader in an atmosphere inseparable from the corruption of dictatorial power. The historical—or pseudohistorical—details in this fiction, like those by other Magical Realists in this genre, matter far less than the devastating portrayal of the pervasive rottenness in which corrupted and corrupters alike must live: the vicious competition among the dictator's lieutenants and their shameless servility in his presence; the casual resort to torture in sniffing out conspiracies real and imagined; the "executions" carried out by the thugs the regime finds ample reasons to employ; the opportunities to gratify the ruler's greed for money, property, and women; the unchecked nepotism that makes his family the beneficiaries of scandalous largesse; not to overlook the demagogic appeals to the populace—more circuses than bread—that turn the professional classes, the merchants, and the poor too, into the accomplices of the despot.

The *caudillos*, and the regimes they establish and ruthlessly defend, are far from all alike. But the curse of existence under their rule is always the death of reason, the sheer unpredictability of life. With no constitution to rein him in, or with a constitution cynically ignored on his orders, no one, the millionaire like the beggar, can make any rational decisions. Honesty, loyalty, hard work, reward for merit—these traditional guideposts have been erased or so disfigured that they have become illegible. The will of the *caudillo* is law; hence trust is the first casualty under his heel. Paranoia becomes endemic, in a way normal. Not even the leader can escape it. The saying that even paranoiacs have enemies is far from a mere joke: the dictator has good reasons to be suspicious of everyone and everything.

It is not immediately clear why the author should call *The Autumn of the Patriarch* "a poem about the solitude of power," for it is an elliptical statement: the solitude of which he speaks is the lot of all. To the extent that García Márquez succeeds in making his argument persuasive, employing literary conceits that no historian could, or should want to, emulate, he has written a novel that is profoundly historical. With its essential veracity, it becomes a creditable ally of the most trenchant history of Trujillo's dictatorship in Santo Domingo or Pinochet's rule over Chile. In short: in the hands of a major novelist, a fiction can make history, in both meanings of that expression.

NOTES

C.D.—Charles Dickens

G.F.—Gustave Flaubert

T.M.—Thomas Mann

PROLOGUE

[p. 17] *had joined the Realist party*: See *Flaubert and Turgenev: A Friendship in Letters. The Complete Correspondence*, trans. and ed. Barbara Beaumont (1985), 37.

[p. 19] *"That is everything: the love of Art"*: G.F. to Louise Colet (August 30, 1846). *Correspondance*, ed. Jean Bruneau, 4 vols. so far (1973–), I, 321.

[p. 19] *"The reality . . . separates the world of reality from that of art"*: T.M., "Bilse und ich," *Gesammelte Werke in zwölf Bänden* (1960–74; cited hereafter as *Werke*) X, 12.

[p. 20] *"Two and a half years later"*: T.M., *Buddenbrooks. Verfall einer Familie* (1901; ed. 1981), 51 [Part II, ch. 1].

[p. 20] *"He traveled"*: G.F., *Education sentimentale. Oeuvres*, ed. A. Thibaudet and R. Dumesnil, 2 vols. (1951–52), II, 448 [Part III, ch. 6].

[p. 23] *"our wet nurse makes herself felt"*: G.F. to his mother (November 24, 1850). *Correspondance*, I, 711–12.

[p. 24] *"root out everything else"*: C.D., *Hard Times. For These Times* (1854; ed. David Craig, 1969), 47 [ch. 1].

[p. 24] *"A man of realities"*: Ibid., 48 [ch. 2].

[p. 27] *"must be set against each other"*: Hilary Mantel, *A Place of Greater Safety* (1992; ed. 1998), x.

[p. 31] *to master the traumas of her life*: For this narrow interpretation, see Theodore J. Jacobs, rapporteur, "Trauma and Mastery Through Art: The Life and Work of George Eliot," *Journal of Applied Pyschoanalytic Studies*, I, 4 (October 1999), 959–60.

[pp. 32–33] *"on or about December 1910 . . . that is left out"*: Virginia Woolf, "Mr. Bennett and Mrs. Brown" (1924): *The Captain's Death Bed and Other Essays* (1950), 91, 98, 90, 97.

ONE

[p. 38] *"Combustion is an* impossibility": G.H. Lewes, open letter to the *Leader*, February 3, 1853. *Dickens: The Critical Heritage*, ed. Philip Collins (1971), 273.

[p. 38] *"I took pains to investigate the subject"*: C.D., *Bleak House* (1854; ed. Stephen Gill, 1996), Preface, 6.

[p. 38] *"most unreal fantastical personage possible"*: (W.M. Thackeray), *Fraser's Magazine* (August 1840). *Dickens: Critical Heritage*, 46.

[p. 38] *"IT IS TRUE"*: C.D., *Bleak House*, Preface, 6.

[p. 39] *"singularly unlike that great original"*: C.D. to John Forster (March 9 [?], 1852). *The Letters of Charles Dickens*, ed. Madeline House, Graham Story, et al., 11 vols. so far (1965–), VI, 623.

[p. 40] *"in all else it is the Life itself"*: C.D. to Mrs. Richard Watson (September 21, 1853). *Letters*, VII, 154.

[p. 40] *"and so I of mine with you"*: C.D. to Leigh Hunt (early November 1853). Ibid, 460.

[p. 40] *"I did not fancy that you would ever recognize it"*: C.D. to Leigh Hunt. Ibid.

[p. 41] *"a great (and dirty) city"*: C.D., *Bleak House*, 11 [ch. 1].

[p. 41] "*the Lord High Chancellor in his High Court of Chancery*": Ibid., 12 [ch. 1].

[p. 41] "*The law . . . is an ass—a idiot*": C.D., *The Adventures of Oliver Twist* (1838; ed. Humphry House, 1949), 399 [ch. 51].

[p. 41] "*fog had even got into the family parlour*": "A Crisis in the Affairs of Mr. John Bull, as Related by Mrs. Bull to the Children," *Household Words*, November 23, 1850. *The Works of Charles Dickens*, National Library Edition, 40 vols. (1902–08). *Miscellaneous Papers, Plays and Poems*, XVIII, 215.

[p. 42] "*JARNDYCE AND JARNDYCE*": C.D., *Bleak House*, 13 [ch. 1].

[p. 45] "*I had always rather a noticing way*": Ibid., 24 [ch. 3].

[p. 46] "*the best wife that ever a man had*": Ibid., 891 [ch. 64].

[p. 46] "*Nothing, nothing*": Ibid.

[p. 46] "*some of the best things in the book*": (John Forster), *Examiner*, October 8, 1853. *Dickens: Critical Heritage*, 291.

[p. 46] "*monstrous failures*": G.H. Lewes, review of vol. I of John Forster's life of Dickens, *Fortnightly Review* (February 1872). Ibid., 574.

[pp. 46–47] "*superintending the jam pots at Bleak House*": George Brimley, *Spectator*, September 24, 1853. Ibid., 285.

[p. 47] "*like a bale of goods*": Anon., *Bentley's Miscellany* (October 1853). Ibid., 289.

[p. 48] *his "favourite child*": C.D., Preface to the Charles Dickens Edition (1869), *The Personal History of David Copperfield* (1850; ed. Trevor Blount, 1966), 47.

[p. 48] "*wisdom and self-sacrificing good*": John Forster, *The Life of Charles Dickens*, 2 vols. (1872–74), II, 133.

[p. 48] "*the real legless angel of Victorian romance*": George Orwell, "Charles Dickens" (1939). *A Collection of Essays by George Orwell* (1954), 109.

[p. 49] "*the greatest of superficial novelists*": Henry James, "Our Mutual Friend," *Nation*, December 21, 1865. *The Critical Muse: Selected Literary Criticism*, ed. Roger Gard (1987), 52.

[p. 50] "*the cause of his decline!*": C.D., *David Copperfield*, 429 [ch. 25].

[p. 52] "*made her frown all her life*": C.D., *Bleak House*, 24 [ch. 3].

[p. 52] "*It would have been far better . . . You are set apart*": Ibid., 25–26 [ch. 3].

[p. 53] *"win some love to myself if I could"*: Ibid., 27 [ch. 3].

[p. 55] *"was warm for my being sent back"*: Forster, *Life of Dickens*, I, 38.

[p. 56] *"She had not a single fault"*: C.D. to Richard Johns (May 31, 1837). *Letters*, I, 263.

[p. 57] *"smashed, squelched, and utterly undone"*: C.D. to John Forster (January 18, 1844). *Letters*, IV, 24.

[p. 58] *"stinging in the last degree"*: C.D. to John Forster (October–November, 1846). Ibid., IV, 651.

[p. 59] *"Tom has his revenge"*: C.D., *Bleak House*, 654–58 [ch. 46].

[p. 59] *"has nowhere in all his work excelled"*: (Henry Fothergill Chorley), review in the *Atheneum*, September 17, 1853. *Dickens: Critical Heritage*, 279.

[p. 60] *"more than half-suffocated"*: C.D., "The Verdict for Drouet," *Household Words*, April 21, 1849. *The Works of Charles Dickens*, XVIII, 93.

[p. 60] *"the happy infants under his paternal charge"*: C.D., "The Paradise at Tooting," *Household Words*, January 20, 1849. Ibid., 81–82.

[p. 61] *"We are the victims of prejudice"*: C.D., *Bleak House*, 854 [ch. 60].

[p. 62] *"neglecting their children and household etc."*: John Stuart Mill to Harriet Taylor (March 20, 1854). *Collected Works of John Stuart Mill*, ed. J.M. Robson, et al., 33 vols (1963–91), XIV, 199.

[pp. 62–63] *"We aspire to live . . . inherent in the human breast"*: C.D., "Address in the first number of 'Household Words'" (March 30, 1850). *The Works of Charles Dickens*, XVIII, 113.

[p. 63]: *"for a world without an ism"*: C.D. to Mrs. Talfourd (April 27, 1844). *Letters*, IV, 114.

[p. 63] *"sentimental radicalism"*: (Walter Bagehot), "Charles Dickens," *National Review* (October 1856), in *Literary Studies*, 3 vols. (1895; ed. 1910), II, 157.

[p. 64] *"making stupendous fools of themselves"*: C.D. to W. H. Wills (August 10, 1851). *Letters*, VI, 457.

[p. 66] *"HOW NOT TO DO IT"*: C.D., *Little Dorrit* (1857; ed. John Holloway, 1967), 145 [ch. 10].

[p. 66] *"an engine drawing no water"*: (James Fitzjames Stephen), "The Licence of Modern Novelists" (review of *Little Dorrit*), *Edinburgh Review* (July 1857). *Dickens: Critical Heritage*, 369–70.

[p. 68] *"Foodle to act with Goodle"*: C.D., *Bleak House,* 173 [ch. 12].

[p. 68] *One close reader*: George H. Ford, *Dickens and His Readers* (1955).

TWO

[p. 73] *"For two days I have been . . . tales of shipwrecks and buccaneers"*: G.F. to Louise Colet (March 3, 1852). *Correspondance,* II, 55–56.

[p. 74] *"the temple of Astarte"*: G.F. to Jules Duplan (May 10 [?], 1857). Ibid., 713.

[p. 74] *"on which I have taken notes"*: G.F. to Jules Duplan (after May 28, 1857). Ibid., 726.

[p. 74] *"formidable archaeological labor"*: G.F. to Jules Duplan (May 10 [?], 1857). Ibid., 713.

[p. 74] *"about a hundred"*: G.F. to Jules Duplan (July 26, 1857). Ibid., 747.

[p. 75] *"But art above everything!"*: G.F. to his niece Caroline (March 9, 1868). *Correspondance,* III, 729.

[p. 75] *"too truthful"*: G.F. to Louis Bonenfant (December 12, 1856). *Correspondance,* II, 652.

[p. 76] *"the most broken-down barrel organ of all"*: Charles Baudelaire, "Madame Bovary par Gustave Flaubert," *L'Artiste,* October 18, 1857. *Oeuvres complètes,* ed. Y. G. Le Dantec and Claude Pichois (1961), 651.

[p. 77] *"moved by my own writing"*: G.F. to Louise Colet (April 24, 1852). *Correspondance,* II, 76.

[p. 78] *vomited up his dinner*: G.F. to Hippolyte Taine (November 20 [?], 1866). Ibid., III, 562.

[p. 78] *"one ends up catching it"*: G.F. to Louise Colet (June 28, 1853). Ibid., II, 367.

[p. 78] *"I am bursting with it"*: G.F. to Edma Roger des Genettes (April 15 [?], 1875). Ibid., IV, 920.

[p. 79] *"I find you on every hand"*: Charles-Augustin Sainte-Beuve, "Madame Bovary, par M. Gustave Flaubert" (May 4, 1857). *Causeries du Lundi,* 15 vols. (1850–80), XIII, 363.

[p. 80] *"the first of all qualities"*: G.F. to Charles Baudelaire (July 13, 1857). *Correspondance,* II, 744.

[p. 80] *"the demolition of romanticism!"*: G.F. to Edmond and Jules de Goncourt (August 12, 1865). Ibid., III, 454.

[p. 80] *"if you will, crusty, old romantic"*: G.F. to Charles-Augustin Sainte-Beuve (May 5, 1857). Ibid., II, 710.

[p. 81] *"first style and then Truth"*: G.F. to Louis Bonenfant (December 12, 1856). Ibid., 652.

[p. 81] *"but not its religion"*: G.F. to Louise Colet (January 11, 1847). Ibid., I, 425.

[p. 82] *"not even any social convictions"*: G.F. to Louise Colet (April 26, 1853). Ibid., II, 316.

[p. 82] *"the hair shirt that scratches his belly"*: G.F. to Louise Colet (April 24, 1852). Ibid., 75.

[p. 82] "The artist must elevate everything!": G.F. to Louise Colet (June 20, 1853). Ibid., 362.

[p. 82] *"but does not see"*: G.F. to Louise Colet (December 9, 1852). Ibid., 294.

[p. 83]: *"I would burst with fear"*: G.F. to Louise Colet (October 26, 2852). Ibid., 174.

[p. 83]: *"we are stuck in first-rate shit!"*: G.F. to Louis Bouilhet (May 30, 1855). Ibid., 576.

[p. 83] *"no idea that is not stale"*: G.F. to Maxime du Camp (beginning of July, 1852). Ibid., 121.

[p. 83] *"gives me an appetite for suicide"*: G.F. to Louise Colet (June 20, 1853). Ibid., 357.

[p. 83]: *"it has no use for it at present"*: G.F. to Louise Colet (April 24, 1852). Ibid., 76.

[p. 84] "What merchants! What dull imbeciles!": G.F. to Louise Colet (April 24, 1852). Ibid., 576.

[p. 84] *"have I been choked by such disgust"*: G.F. to his niece Caroline (October 25, 1872). Ibid., IV, 593.

[p. 84] *"copious and bitter, I promise you"*: G.F. to Ernest Feydeau (October 28, 1872). Ibid., 596.

[p. 84] "messieurs *the working people*": G.F. to George Sand (April 30, 1871). Ibid., IV, 313–14.

[p. 85] "*predictable dessert after the monotony of dinner*": *Madame Bovary. Moeurs de province* (1857). Gustave Flaubert, *Oeuvres*, 2 vols., ed. Albert Thibaudet and René Dumesnil (1951–52), I, 331 [Part 1, ch. 7].

[p. 85] "*the radiance of the tapers*": Ibid., 323 [I, 6].

[p. 86] "*the bottom of her soul*": Ibid.

[p. 86] "*looking for emotions and not scenery*": Ibid., 324 [I, 6].

[p. 86] "*from the distant open country*": Ibid., 325 [I, 6].

[p. 87] "*the happiness of which she had dreamed*": Ibid., 327 [I, 6].

[p. 89] "*that is to say, everybody*": G.F. to Ernest Feydeau (August 17, 1861). *Correspondance*, III, 170.

[p. 89] "*in the back of the shop*": G.F. to Louise Colet (April 30, 1847). Ibid., I, 452.

[p. 89] "*I have reflected . . . every time I have attempted it*": G.F. to Albert LePoittevin (June 17, 1845). Ibid., 241.

[p. 90] "*Bite me, bite me! Do you remember?*": G.F. to Louise Colet (September 10, 1846). Ibid., 334.

[p. 90] "*I sucked her furiously*": G.F. to Louis Bouilhet (March 13, 1950). Ibid., 607.

[p. 90] "*What kisses I send you!*": Caroline Flaubert to G.F. (November 10, 1842). *Correspondance*, I, 126.

[p. 90] "*when one lights the lamps*": G.F. to Alfred LePoittevin (May 1, 1845). Ibid., 227.

[p. 91] "*Maria had a child . . . this kiss would give me*": G.F., *Mémoires d'un fou* (1839; publ. 1900–01). *Mémoires d'un fou, Novembre et autres texts de jeunesse*, ed. Yvan Leclerc (1991), 292–93.

[p. 92] "ma toujours aimée": G.F. to Elisa Schlésinger (May 28, 1872). *Correspondance*, IV, 529.

[p. 93] "*Don't touch it!*": G.F., *Madame Bovary*, 518–19 [III, 2].

[p. 93] "*he knew them very well*": Ibid., 410 [II, 7].

[p. 94] "*something pliant and corrupt*": Ibid., 466 [II, 12].

[p. 94] "*he f——d her to death*": G.F., *Madame Bovary, nouvelle version*, with unpublished sketches and drafts, ed. Jean Pommier and Gabrielle Leleu (1949), 93.

[p. 94] "*voluptuousness for her*": G.F., *Madame Bovary*, 466 [II, 12].

[p. 95] "*feet dressed in patent-leather*": Ibid., 502 [III, 1].

[p. 95] *"by very eminent critics"*: (James Fitzjames Stephen), *Saturday Review*, July 11, 1857.

[p. 96] *"the condition of French society"*: Ibid., 57.

[p. 97] *"I am being too truthful"*: G.F. to Louis Bonenfant (December 12, 1856). *Correspondance*, II, 652.

[p. 97] *"demolish the* Revue de Paris": G.F. to Edmond Pagnerre (December 31, 1856). Ibid., 656.

[p. 97] "political matter": G.F. to Achille Flaubert (January 1, 1857). Ibid., 657.

[p. 97] *"something invisible and tenacious"*: G.F. to Achille Flaubert (January 16, 1857). Ibid., 667.

[p. 98] *"the times of Napoleon III?"*: G.F. to Louise Colet (April 22, 1854). Ibid., 557.

[p. 98] *"even when he was on a throne"*: Alfred Cobban, *A History of Modern France*, vol. 2, *1799–1871* (1961; 2nd ed. 1965), 162.

[p. 99] *"sometimes into those of married women"*: Ernest Pinard, "Réquisitoire" [prosecutor's plea in the *Ministère Public* vs. Gustave Flaubert, January 28, 1857]. G.F., *Oeuvres*, I, 631–32.

[p. 100] *"in all its nudity, in all its crudity"*: Ibid., 627.

[p. 100] the *"poetry of adultery"*: Ibid., 623, 624, 628.

[p. 101] "Bovarystes enragées": G.F. to Achille Flaubert (January 6, 1857). *Correspondance*, II, 662.

[p. 101] *"rather a moral book"*: (Fitzjames Stephen), *Saturday Review*, July 11, 1857.

[p. 101] *"like drinking, eating, pissing, etc."*: G.F. to Louise Colet (April 24, 1852). *Correspondance*, II, 77.

[p. 102] *"the taut watered silk"*: G.F., *Madame Bovary*, 307 [I, 2].

[p. 103] *"with little thrusts"*: Ibid., 311 [I, 3].

[p. 103] "elle s'abandonna": Ibid., 438 [II, 9].

[p. 104] *"with a long shudder"*: Ibid., 548–49 [III, 6].

[p. 104] *"I have a lover!"*: Ibid., 439 [II, 9].

[p. 104] *"all the platitudes of marriage"*: Ibid., 556 [III, 6].

[p. 105] *"by choosing and exaggerating"*: G.F. to Hippolyte Taine (June 14, 1867). *Correspondance*, III, 655.

[p. 106] *"I'll avenge myself!"*: G.F. to Louise Colet (June 28, 1853). Ibid., II, 367.

[p. 107] *"as in strangulated hernias"*: G.F. to Louis Bouilhet (September 30, 1855). Ibid., 597–600.

[p. 107] *"to dissect is to take revenge"*: G.F. to George Sand (December 18, 1867). *Correspondance*, III, 711.

[p. 107] *"which distorts their ideas"*: Charles Baudelaire, "Madame Bovary, par Gustave Flaubert." *Oeuvres*, 651.

[p. 109] *"Let's hope so!"*: G.F. to Edma Roger des Genettes (October 30, 1856). Ibid., II, 644.

[p. 109] *"the cross of the Legion of Honor"*: G.F., *Madame Bovary*, 611 [III, 11].

THREE

[p. 113] *"elevation of the moment"*: T.M., "Der französische Einfluss" (1904), *Werke*, X, 837.

[pp. 113–14] *"recorder of good dinners"*: Ibid.

[p. 114] *"my receptive youth"*: T.M., "Bilse und ich" (1906), *Werke*, X, 11.

[p. 114] *"eleven hundred pages long"*: T.M. to Martha Hartmann (April 23, 1903). *Thomas Mann. Teil I, 1889–1917*, ed. James Wysling, with Marianne Fischer, 3 vols. (1975–81). I, 37.

[p. 114] *"It was Number 52"*: T.M. to Julius Bab (October 5, 1910). Ibid., 45.

[p. 115] "I thought . . . there would be nothing more": T.M., *Buddenbrooks. Verfall einer Familie* (1901), *Werke*, I, 523 [Part VIII, ch. 7].

[p. 117] *"it concerned me very little"*: T.M., *Betrachtungen eines Unpolitischen, Werke*, XII, 145.

[p. 120] *"without being German?"*: Ibid., 73.

[p. 121] *"self-disposal*—Selbstabschaffungsplänen": T.M. to Heinrich Mann (February 13, 1901). *Briefe*, ed. Erika Mann, 3 vols. (1962–65), I, 25.

[p. 121] *"metaphysics, music, and adolescent eroticism"*: T.M. to Heinrich Mann (March 7, 1901). Ibid., 27.

[p. 122] *"With typhoid, things proceed as follows"*: T.M., *Buddenbrooks*, 781 [XI, 3].

[p. 124] *"ashamed beyond all bounds"*: Ibid., 146 [III, 9].

[p. 124] *"sealed the engagement"*: Ibid., 163 [III, 14].

[pp. 124–25] *"wonderfully pretty"*: Ibid., 168 [III, 15].

[p. 125] *"one is borne along"*: Ibid., 170 [III, 15].

[p. 125] "L'année la plus heureuse de ma vie": Ibid., 56 [II, 1].

[p. 126] *"God had entrusted to him"*: Ibid.

[pp. 126–27] *"As you know . . . in a position to make a* partie": Ibid., 114 [III, 4].

[p. 127] *"I assure you"*: Ibid., 105 [III, 2].

[p. 127] *"Are you satisfied with me?"*: Ibid., 166 [III, 14].

[p. 128] *"redoubled his love"*: Ibid., 233 [IV, 10].

[p. 129] *"contributed to my enthusiasm"*: Ibid., 290 [V, 7].

[p. 129] *"captivating and mysterious beauty"*: Ibid., 272 [V, 8].

[p. 130] *"tacit, deep mutual intimacy"*: Ibid., 624 [X, 5].

[p. 130] *"you will never understand anything"*: Ibid., 509 [VIII, 7].

[p. 131] *"he sometimes groaned softly"*: Ibid., 647 [X, 5].

[pp. 133–34] *"And now came the finale . . . rapture played about his mouth"*: Ibid., 507 [VIII, 6].

[p. 135] *"walls of flame collapsing into themselves"*: Ibid., 750 [XI, 2].

[p. 137] *"a friendship understood, reciprocated, worthwhile"*: T.M. to Heinrich Mann (March 7, 1901). *Briefe*, I, 27.

[p. 137] *"like a treasure"*: T.M. to Hermann Lange (March 19, 1955). Ibid., 387.

[p. 139] *"my scorn and my accusations"*: T.M. to Otto Grautoff (July 27, 1897). Hermann Kurzke, *Thomas Mann. Das Leben als Kunstwerk* (1999), 85–86.

[p. 139] *"an expression of my sexual inversion"*: T.M., *Tagebuch*, September 17, 1919.

[p. 140] *"I am telling the truth"*: T.M., *Buddenbrooks*, 580 [IX, 2].

[p. 141] *"with joy and satisfaction"*: Ibid., 612 [X, 1].

[p. 142] *"Have I hoped . . . I shall live!"*: Ibid., 659 [X, 5].

[p. 142] *"an odd and ridiculous role"*: Ibid., 654 [X, 5].

[p. 143] *"merchants of the Holy Roman Empire"*: *Betrachtungen eines Unpolitischen, Werke*, XII, 115.

[p. 144] *"I am more attached to* Tonio Kröger": T.M. to Jean Schlumberger (September 18, 1931). *Briefe,* I, 306.

[p. 144] *"at home in neither":* T.M., *Tonio Kröger* (1903), *Werke,* VIII, 337.

[p. 144] *"the human, the living, the common":* Ibid., 338.

[p. 146] *"sublime* revenge *on his experience":* T.M., "Bilse und ich," *Werke,* X, 20.

EPILOGUE

[p. 150] *"would not stay for an answer":* Francis Bacon, "Of Truth" (1625). Opening sentence in *Essays,* many editions.

[p. 150] *"which creates this beautiful world":* Sir Karl Popper made this point several times. See, for instance, "Two Faces of Common Sense: An Argument for Commonsense Realism and Against the Commonsense Theory of Knowledge," *Objective Knowledge: An Evolutionary Approach* (1972; rev. ed. 1975). 41.

[p. 151] *"what only the novel can say":* Milan Kundera, "Dialogue on the Art of the Novel" (1983). *The Art of the Novel* (1986; trans. Linda Asher, 1988), 36.

[p. 151] *"no social or political thought could ever tell us":* Milan Kundera, "Somewhere Behind" (1984). Ibid., 117, (italics in the original).

[p. 152] *"I could spell out with conviction":* C. Vann Woodward, *Thinking Back: The Perils of Writing History* (1986), 34.

[p. 153] *"multiple possibilities of alternative narrations":* Simon Schama, *Dead Certainties (Unwarranted Speculations)* (1991), 320.

[pp. 153–54] *"belong to the order of discourse":* Hayden White, "Historical Emplotment and the Problem of Truth," in *Probing the Limits of Representation,* ed. Saul Friedlander (1992), 37.

[p. 155] *"character and prejudices of its narrator":* Schama, *Dead Certainties (Unwarranted Speculations),* 322.

[p. 157] *"Objectivity is not neutrality":* Thomas L. Haskell, "Objectivity is not Neutrality: Rhetoric versus Practice in Peter Novick's *That Noble Dream,"* in *Objectivity Is Not Neutrality: Explanatory Schemes in History* (1998).

[p. 160] *"all the dictators in the history of man"*: Gabriel García Márquez, 1977 interview, in Michael Palencia-Roth, "Intertextualities: Three Metaphors of Myth in *The Autumn of the Patriarch.*" *Gabriel García Márquez and the Powers of Fiction*, ed. Julio Ortega with Claudia Elliott (1988), 35–36.

[p. 160] *"especially those from the Caribbean"*: Gabriel García Márquez, *El olor de la guayaba: Conversacion con Plinio Apuleyo Mendoza* (1982). Raymond L. Williams, *Gabriel García Márquez* (1984), 111.

[p. 160] *"the phantoms of Latin America"*: Gabriel García Márquez, "The Solitude of Latin America." Nobel Prize address (1982), in *Gabriel García Márquez: New Readings*, ed. Bernard McGuirk and Richard Carwell (1987), 208.

[p. 161] *"never had a moment of serenity"*: García Márquez, "Solitude of Latin America," *New Readings*, 208.

[p. 162] *"eternity had come to an end"*: Gabriel García Márquez, *The Autumn of the Patriarch* (1975; trans. Gregory Rabassa, 1976), 255.

[p. 164] *"a poem about the solitude of power"*: Gabriel García Márquez, *El olor de la guayaba*, Williams, *Gabriel García Márquez*, 121.

BIBLIOGRAPHICAL NOTES

These notes do not pretend to be complete; they do not even exhaust all the materials I have consulted. I have confined myself to writings that have provided reliable information, influenced or intrigued me, or have prompted me to dissent.

PROLOGUE

The indispensable text that takes Realism all the way from Homer to Virginia Woolf is Erich Auerbach's classic *Mimesis: The Representation of Reality in Western Literature* (1946; trans. Willard R. Trask, 1953), a masterpiece of clarity and analytical power. René Wellek has a characteristically scholarly essay, "The Concept of Realism in Literary Scholarship" (1960), in *Concepts of Criticism* (1963). Wellek's great *A History of Modern Criticism*, 8 vols. (1955–91), has much to say about Realism in vols. 3 and 4. George Levine, *The Realistic Imagination: English Fiction from Frankenstein to Lady Chatterley* (1981), ably concentrates on British writers. *Documents of Modern Literary Realism*, ed. George J. Becker (1963), is a highly informative collection of relevant statements from Vissarion Belinsky to Erich Heller, Gustave Flaubert to

Marcel Proust, Emile Zola to Philip Rahv, some of them of generous length and covering a wide waterfront. *The Age of Realism*, ed. F. W. J. Hemmings, surveys Realist fiction from its eighteenth-century beginnings to its decline in the Modernist age. I have learned much from *The Monster in the Mirror: Studies in Nineteenth-Century Realism*, ed. D. A. Williams (1978), with clear, authoritative essays on nine novels including, among others, Balzac, *Lost Illusions*; Flaubert, *Sentimental Education*; W. D. Howells, *The Rise of Silas Lapham*; and Theodor Fontane, *Effi Briest*. Wayne C. Booth, *The Rhetoric of Fiction* (1961), includes Realism in its survey. And Harry Levin, *The Gates of Horn* (1963), with lengthy essays on Stendhal, Balzac, Flaubert, Zola, and Proust, is Levin's authoritative statement about French Realism, on which he had labored for decades.

There are relatively few texts that examine the historical novel as a genre, to see how imaginary gardens with real toads in them must fare. A. S. Byatt has mobilized her sharp intellect and extensive reading in some openly experimental lectures, *On Histories and Stories: Selected Essays* (2001); to my mind, her explorations are somewhat compromised by a weakness for certain postmodernists, for unhistorical historians, thus bringing fiction and history into far closer proximity than I think it right to do. Georg Lukács, *The Historical Novel* (1937; trans. Hannah and Stanley Mitchell, 1962), naturally sees the evolution of the genre from a materialist standpoint; still, his comments on individual novels are worth considering. Morroe Berger, looking at novels from a sociologist's perspective in *Real and Imagined Worlds: The Novel and Social Science* (1977), has a chapter (7) on fiction and history. Moving from the collective to the individual, Allan Conrad Christensen, *Edward Bulwer-Lytton: The Fiction of New Regions* (1976), devotes chapter 5 to an analysis of an author who (after Sir Walter Scott) helped to make historical novels both respectable and trendy. Alice Chandler, *A Dream of Order: The Medieval Ideal in Nineteenth-Century Literature* (1970), shows how medievalism became pervasive in Victorian England, especially after Scott had exercised his immense influence—and not in Britain alone. By far the most persuasive study of Scott, an invitation to read, or reread, the old master, is Alexander Welsh, *The Hero of the Waverly Novels* (1963; 2nd ed. 1992).

Scott was, to many European novelists, the father of historical Realism. Peter Demetz, *Formen des Realismus: Theodor Fontane. Kritische Untersuchungen* (1964; 2nd ed. 1966), starts with Scott and traces his impact on German Realism in detail. Eda Sagarra, *Tradition and Revolution: German Literature and Society 1830–1890* (1971), observes that under Scott's influence, German historical novelists became more socially acceptable—more *salonfähig*—than ever before. For Scott and the historical novel in France, see M. G. Hutt and Christophe Campos, "Romanticism and History," in *French Literature and Its Background*, vol. 4, *The Early Nineteenth Century*, ed. John Cruickshank (1969), 97–113, esp. 100–06.

For Tolstoy's view of history, there is above all Isaiah Berlin's famous essay, *The Hedgehog and the Fox* 91953). R. F. Christian, *Tolstoy's "War and Peace": A Study* (1962), is very much to the point. Christian has also edited Tolstoy's *Letters* in two volumes (1982) that contain a number of pertinent observations. Aylmer Maude's life of Tolstoy, 2 vols. (1930), retains its authority.

O N E : Charles Dickens in *Bleak House*

There are innumerable editions of Dickens's works, more or less complete, more or less dependable. Two recent collections, reasonably priced and easily available, are The New Oxford Illustrated Dickens, 21 vols. (1947–58), and the individual volumes in the Penguin Classics. Both are equipped with helpful notes and introductions. For *Bleak House*, I have used Stephen Gill's edition (1996). The splendid Pilgrim Edition of *The Letters of Charles Dickens*, almost complete with eleven bulky, fully annotated volumes so far, ed. Madeline House, Graham Story, Kathleen Tillotson, et al. (1965–), proved, in a word, indispensable. For Dickens's periodical writings, see above all *Household Words*, accessible in several collected works. *Charles Dickens's Uncollected Writings from "Household Words" 1850–1859*, ed. Harry Stone (1968), makes available several pieces that Dickens usually wrote with a co-author. There is a convenient edition of *Sketches by Boz* (1836–50), intro. by Peter Ackroyd, which contains Dickens's prefaces to the several editions of this collection.

Among the numerous biographies of Charles Dickens, the first, by his intimate John Forster—*The Life of Charles Dickens*, 2 vols. (1872–74 and several later editions)—is still much worth reading for the verdicts, and the delicacy, of a close and not uncritical friend judging the genius whom the author knew so well. Among modern lives, Edgar Johnson's diligent *Charles Dickens, His Tragedy and Triumph*, 2 vols. (1952), is usually considered the standard life. It is reliable though excessively admiring, and its essays on individual novels are superficial and a little preachy. Fred Kaplan, *Dickens: A Biography* (1988), is the most appealing recent life that is wholly at home in the modern scholarship.

Alexander Welsh has written several highly original, in the best sense suggestive, elegant essays, particularly *From Copyright to Copperfield: The Identity of Dickens* (1987), and *Dickens Redressed: The Art of "Bleak House" and "Hard Times"* (2000). I used the excellent Norton Critical Edition of *Bleak House*, ed. George Ford and Sylvère Monod (1977); and Susan Shatto, *The Companion to "Bleak House,"* (1988), an informative valuable survey. Esther Summerson, much maligned across a century and a half, has enlisted a brave handful of defenders; most to my purposes Alex Zwerdling, in a convincing psychoanalytic study, "Esther Summerson Rehabilitated," PMLA, LXXXVIII (1973), 429–39. William S. Holdsworth, *Charles Dickens as a Legal Historian* (1928), offers some serious reservations concerning Dickens's caricature of the Court of Chancery. "The Bench," chapter 8 in Philip Collins, *Dickens and Crime* (1962; 2nd ed., 1964), sustains and adds to these criticisms.

Dickens the writer has elicited some exceptionally rewarding scholarship. Humphry House's brilliant *The Dickens World* (1941; 2nd ed. 1942) establishes that Dickens indiscriminately took his imaginative material from several decades of early nineteenth-century England and wrote (as I document in some detail) as an impulsive reformer. Philip Collins, in addition to *Dickens and Crime*, has an equally impressive study, *Dickens and Education* (1963; rev. 1964). John Butt and Kathleen Tillotson, *Dickens at Work* (1957), is a carefully detailed exploration of Dickens's methods of writing and rewriting. Michael Slater's substantial *Dickens and Women* (1983) traces in rewarding detail Dickens's involvement with women both real and imagined. Two books that well complement one another track down the reception of Dickens through the decades: George H. Ford, *Dickens and His Readers: Aspects of Novel Criticism Since 1836* (1955), and *The Dickens Critics*, ed. George H. Ford and Lauriat Lane, Jr. (1961), the latter offering almost three dozen well-selected literary verdicts. *Dickens: The Critical Heritage*, ed. Philip Collins (1971), which offers sizable passages from a wide spectrum of contemporary and later reviews, was open on my desk as I wrote this book. It shows that Dickens criticism was a heavy industry even in his lifetime.

Among the mass of contemporary appraisals, Walter Bagehot, "Charles Dickens" (1856), in *Literary Studies*, 3 vols. (1895), stands out. Amid the flood of twentieth-century commentary, George Orwell, "Charles Dickens" (1939), reprinted in *A Collection of Essays by George Orwell* (1954), 55–111, is typical for its author—both vigorous and exhilarating. Harry Stone, *The Night Side of Dickens: Cannibalism, Passion, Necessity* (1994), looks rather eccentric, but makes important suggestions about the darker Dickens. F. R. and Q. D. Leavis, *Dickens the Novelist* (1970), is not without interest, even though its judgments strike me as perverse, doctrinaire, and self-important. In *The Intellectual Life of the British Working Classes* (2001), Jonathan Rose documents Dickens's vast popularity among the "lower orders."

TWO: Gustave Flaubert in *Madame Bovary*

The standard source for Flaubert's writings has long remained the so-called Conard edition, 12 vols. (1910–54), even though Benjamin F. Bart, who has consulted the original manuscripts, has pointed out that its text, "although usually the best available, is frequently unreliable"—*Flaubert* (1967), 746. I have instead relied on *Oeuvres*, 2 vols., ed. Albert Thibaudet and René Dumesnil (1951–52), which is well edited for what it covers, but unfortunately omits all of Flaubert's youthful writings (a significant and indefensible editorial decision) and other minor works. This oversight can be partially made up with a handy one-volume collection, *Flaubert: Mémoires d'un fou, Novembre, et autres textes de jeunesse*, ed. Yvan Leclerc (1991). As for Flaubert's copious, dazzling, absolutely essential correspondence, the Conard edition, just mentioned, has a nine-volume collection (1926–33), to which a four-volume supplement was added in 1954. Fortunately, I could work with Jean Bruneau's beautifully annotated *Correspondance*, whose four volumes so far (1973–98) reach to 1875, five years before Flaubert's death.

I note that all translations from the French (as from the German) are mine, though I have consulted Francis Steegmuller's English-language version of *Madame Bovary*, which is the best, but far freer than my own. *Madame Bovary, nouvelle version*, including unpublished sketches and drafts, ed. Jean Pommier and Gabrielle Leleu (1949), is an eye-opening scholarly triumph. A Norton Critical Edition, *Madame Bovary* (1965), edited by Paul DeMan "with a substantially new translation" by the editor (who bases himself on the late nineteenth-century rendering by Eleanor Marx), is in my judgment stiff and at times unidiomatic; yet this edition has a wide sampling of literary criticism and biographical materials, including excerpts from Flaubert's fascinating early scenarios for the novel (but primly omitting the raunchiest passages, which I quote in the text, about Rodolphe's sexual exploitation of Emma).

Among biographies, Bart's *Flaubert*, mentioned above, is the most substantial. Maurice Nadeau, *Gustave Flaubert, écrivain* (1969; 2nd ed. 1980), is strong on the writings. Francis Steegmuller, *Flaubert and "Madame Bovary": A Double Portrait* (1939; 2nd ed. 1947), is a stylish biography up to and including Flaubert's masterpiece. For a short life, see Philip Spencer, *Flaubert: A Biography* (1952). Jean-Paul Sartre, *The Family Idiot: Gustave Flaubert, 1821–1857*, trans. Carol Cosman, 3 vols. (1972), volubly "psychoanalyzes" the mental evolution of the young Flaubert. How, Sartre asks, did this writer, who showed no signs of homosexual impulses, convert himself into a woman to write his great novel? Of inordinate length, this investigation of a historical neurosis is not without its insights, but essentially an acquired taste that I, for one, did not acquire. (For a pious summary and appreciation of this nearly 3000-page-long treatise, see Hazel E. Barnes, *Sartre & Flaubert* [1981]). In delightful contrast, Victor Brombert's *Flaubert par lui-même* (1971) is far more rewarding, a kind of intellectual (and to me most instructive) biography of Flaubert's mind that interweaves texts drawn from his writings formal and informal with Brombert's lucid comments.

In the steadily growing secondary literature, Brombert, too, stands out with *The Novels of Flaubert: A Study of Themes and Techniques* (1966). For Flaubert's early years, see esp. Jean Bruneau, *Les débuts littéraires de Flaubert, 1831–1845* (1962), and G. M. Mason, *Les écrits de jeunesse de Flaubert* (1961). Interestingly, but not surprisingly, men of letters have frequently turned to *Madame Bovary* for inspiration. See esp. Mario Vargas Llosa, *The Perpetual Orgy: Flaubert and "Madame Bovary"* (1975; trans. Helen Lane, 1986); a hearty declaration of love for the novel and, above all, for its heroine, the book is also an orderly, affectionate exposition of contents and style. I must not forget Julian Barnes's *Flaubert's Parrot* (1984), among the most successful of his novels, amusing and moving alike with its postmodern acrobatic shifts of presentation and style, in which an impassioned Flaubert scholar, who knows his man's life and letters by heart, makes his research into a defense against sadness.

As a general study, F. W. J. Hemmings, *Culture and Society in France,*
1848–1898: Dissidents and Philistines (1971), is exceptionally illuminating.

THREE: Thomas Mann in *Buddenbrooks*

Of the several collected works of Thomas Mann, I have used the
Gesammelte Werke, 12 vols. (1960), with an added supplementary volume (1972). Most of his letters have been published correspondent by
correspondent. The researcher needs them—for example, *Briefwechsel*
mit seinem Verleger Gottfried Bermann Fischer, 1932–1955 (1973),
Hermann Hesse-Thomas Mann: Briefwechsel, ed. Anni Carlsson (1968),
or *Thomas Mann-Heinrich Mann: Briefwechsel 1900–1949*, ed. Hans
Wysling (1968; enlarged ed. 1995)—since the *Briefe*, ed. Erika Mann,
3 vols. (1962–65), though looking bulky, is really thin and excessively
selective. *Thomas Mann*, in the series *Dichter über ihre Dichtungen*, ed.
Hans Wysling with Marianne Fischer, 3 vols. (1975–81), is a valuable,
apparently exhaustive compendium of Mann's comments on his own
work, drawn in part from letters difficult of access.

The stream of biographies during the mid-1980s and after, as Mann's
homoeroticism became, instead of an open secret, a public matter, is
only now beginning to slow down. The most satisfactory of the recent
batch is Hermann Kurzke, *Thomas Mann. Das Leben als Kunstwerk*
(1999), which, unlike several other lives, gives equal weight to life and
work (or, better, properly joins the two). Klaus Harpprecht, *Thomas*
Mann. Eine Biographie (1995), is monumental (over 2,253 pages). In
English, Nigel Hamilton, *The Brothers Mann: The Lives of Heinrich and*
Thomas Mann 1871–1950 and 1875–1955 (1979), skillfully pursues a
lifelong love-hate relationship. Richard Winston's biography, *Thomas*
Mann: The Making of an Artist, 1875–1911 (1981), was unfortunately
cut short by the death of the author. Among shorter lives, Henry Hatfield,
Thomas Mann (1951; rev. ed. 1962), is an intelligent literary study.

For Thomas Mann, the line between biography and criticism is very porous. Hatfield's *From "The Magic Mountain": Mann's Later Masterpieces* (1979) is marked by the author's uncommon common sense. Erich Kahler, *The Orbit of Thomas Mann* (1969), is a series of five linked essays about Mann's increasing engagement in politics by an intellectual who knew Mann well. Kurt Sontheimer, *Thomas Mann und die Deutschen* (1961), soberly explores the same delicate issue, as does Harpprecht, using the same title (1990). Erich Heller, *The Ironic German* (1958), does full justice to Mann's favorite and most famous stance. The least ideologically loaded, least vulgar, of Marxist critiques, Georg Lukàcs, *Essays on Thomas Mann* (1961), trans. Stanley Mitchell, (1964), predictably treats Mann as a bourgeois Realist, though, Lukàcs admits, a Realist of distinction.

EPILOGUE

It is not necessary to document in detail the prevailing consensus among philosophers concerning the dominance of Critical Realism. John Passmore, *A Hundred Years of Philosophy* (1957; 2nd ed., 1966), is admittedly loaded in favor of Anglo-American philosophy and has little use for Continental metaphysics, but does display the strength of the Realist tradition. G. E. Moore's *Philosophical Papers*, brought together in the year of his death (1958), with their powerful common sense, remain eminently worth reading. Karl Popper, whom I quote in the text, stoutly defended Realism all his life. See, for one such defense, *Objective Knowledge: An Evolutionary Approach* (1972; rev. ed. 1985). Bryan Magee's *Popper* (1973) is a short study by a vehement Popperian. A number of J. L. Austen's witty papers speak to a Realist vision, notably "Truth" (1950) and "Unfair to Facts" (read in 1954), both in Austen, *Philosophical Papers*, ed. J. O. Urmson and G. J. Warnock (1961). Thomas Nagel's felicitous philosophical writings on the reality of reality and the potential for objectivity have been important to me; I am particularly indebted to *The*

View from Nowhere (1986) and *The Last Word* (1997). William P. Alston, *A Realist Conception of the Truth* (1996), is technical but rewarding even to an outsider. See also John McDowell, *Mind and World* (1994).

Thomas Kuhn's celebrated essay *The Structure of Scientific Revolutions* (1962), which I quote in the text, was a sensational success beyond the author's wildest dreams. With its seductive notions of shifting paradigms in scientific ideologies, it gave comfort to postmodern subjectivists, who hailed Kuhn as their ally in their assaults on "naive positivists" or "naive realists." This was in part Kuhn's fault, since one could read his short treatise as viewing the history of science not as a story of progress but of successive ways of viewing the past through clouded lenses. Yet his later, carefully qualified writings show that Kuhn never believed in the fairy tale that the observer makes the external world. See *The Essential Tension: Selected Studies in Scientific Tradition and Change* (1977) and *The Road Since Structure: Philosophical Essays, 1970–1993*, ed. James Conent and John Haugeland (2000). Kuhn, it turns out, was not a relativist or a subjectivist.

Anyone looking for a crash course in postmodernist views on history should consult *The Post-Modern History Reader*, ed. Keith Jenkins (1997), which has impartially selected little-known postmoderns and the heavy hitters alike. It even gives houseroom to a few skeptics. Among historians, the leading (and in his own way, most plausible) postmodern theorist is Hayden White. In *Metahistory: The Historical Imagination of Nineteenth-Century Europe* (1973), *Tropics of Discourse* (1978), and *The Content of the Form* (1987), he converts history into a kind of (generally unacknowledged) novel about the past. In the preface to the first of these texts, he tells the reader what to expect: "I treat the historical work as what it most manifestly is: a verbal structure in the form of a narrative prose discourse." The "deep structural content" of history "is generally poetic, and specifically linguistic, in nature . . ." (p. ix). White's master, as he has been for other postmodernists, is (in addition to Friedrich Nietzsche, everyone's favorite in that school of thought) Michel Foucault.

Note esp. Foucault's *The Order of Things: An Archaeology of the Human Sciences* (1966; trans. Alan Sheridan-Smith, 1970); the revealing collection *Power/Knowledge: Selected Interviews and Other Writings, 1972–1977*, ed. C. Gordon, et al. (1980); and his two disastrous ventures into modern cultural history, *Madness and Civilization: A History of Insanity in the Age of Reason* (1964; trans. Richard Howard, 1971), and *Discipline and Punish: The Birth of the Prison* (1975; trans. Alan Sheridan, 1977).* The main trouble with Foucault's postmodern excursions into history is that his psychology is hopelessly reductionist: it is all a matter of power for him, of a half-unintentional conspiracy of the haves against the have-nots. Hadan Sarup, *Post-Structuralism and Post-Modernism* (1988), especially in its much-enlarged second edition (1993), is far more sympathetic to these movements than I am, but attempts a balance and offers summaries of the thought of Jacques Lacan, Jacques Derrida, Jean-François Lyotard, Jean Baudrillard, and others.

In recent years, the literature on Latin-American work has been growing in tandem with an increasing appreciation of its modern exemplars— especially on the Magical Realism of Gabriel García Márquez. For his fiction, see, above all, *Gabriel García Márquez and the Powers of Fiction*, ed. Julio Ortega and Claudia Elliott (1988), esp. Ortega's essay on "Intertextualities: Three Metaphors of Myth in *The Autumn of the Patriarch*." See also *Gabriel García Márquez, New Readings*, ed. Bernard McGuirk and Riarch Caldwell (1987), and Raymond L. Williams, *Gabriel García Márquez* (1984). Perhaps the most satisfactory volume for this burgeoning literature in general is *Latin American Fiction: A Survey*, ed. John King (1987), with essays by some of the leading writers. Gerald Martin, *Journeys Through the Labyrinth: Latin American Fiction in the Twentieth Century* (1989), is a valuable companion.

---

* This is not to say that Foucault got everything wrong. He was among the first to note that, appearances to the contrary, the "sexual discourse" was very rich in the Victorian age.

ACKNOWLEDGMENTS

I presented a first, briefer version of this book as the W. W. Norton Lectures at the Center for Scholars and Writers in the New York Public Library in October 2000. A number of the Center's fellows in the year 2000–2001, notably Walter Frisch, Tony Holden, Anne Mendelson, and Claudia Pierpont, improved the text with their wisdom. An earlier, quite different draft of chapter 3 served as the Robert Stoller Lecture for 1995 at UCLA. Before then, I tried out preliminary ideas for chapters two and three in University Lectures at the University of Wisconsin and the Page-Barbour-Lectures at the University of Virginia. During numerous lunches at the unmatched Yorkside Pizza in New Haven, Doron Ben-Atar and I discussed this text, and I am grateful to him for carefully and constructively reading the complete draft of my manuscript. Bob Weil proved, once again, a most supportive editor, Jason Baskin efficiently ran interference, and Ann Adelman was the kind of copyeditor that most writers only fantasize about. As always, my wife, Ruth, suffered through my chapters version by version, gladly and helpfully.

—PETER GAY
Hamden, Connecticut, and New York City,
January 2002

INDEX